Rethinking Families

Fiona Williams
ESRC CAVA Research Group

ESRC Research Group on Care, Values and the Future of Welfare
(CAVA) at the University of Leeds included:

Fiona Williams (Director), Carol Smart (Deputy Director),
Louise Ackers, Shelley Budgeon, Harriet Churchill,
Alan Deacon, Simon Duncan, Keleigh Groves, Helen Harvey,
Wendy Hollway, Yasmin Hussain, Sarah Irwin, Angela Jackman,
Jennifer Mason, Greg Martin, Steve Mosby, Bren Neale,
Angela Phillips, Sasha Roseneil, Lise Saugeres, Jessica Shipman,
Rebecca Shipman, Darren Smith and Helen Waite.

 CALOUSTE GULBENKIAN FOUNDATION

The Calouste Gulbenkian Foundation from time to time publishes policy papers to assist policy-makers and to engage general debate about matters of current importance. This book fits into discussions about care, families, supportive relationships and work/life balance and what the implications might be for the future.

Published by
Calouste Gulbenkian Foundation
United Kingdom Branch
98 Portland Place
London W1B 1ET
Tel: 020 7908 7604
E-mail: info@gulbenkian.org.uk
Website: www.gulbenkian.org.uk

© 2004 Calouste Gulbenkian Foundation
reprinted 2005

ISBN 1 903080 02 9
    978 190308002 3

British Library Cataloguing-in-Publication Data
A catalogue record for this book is available from the British Library

Designed by Andrew Shoolbred; cover designed by Onvisual,
www.onvisual.com, illustration by Sima Vaziry
Printed by Expression Printers Ltd, IP23 8HH

Distributed by Central Books Ltd, 99 Wallis Road, London E9 5LN
Tel: 0845 458 9911, Fax: 0845 458 9912
E-mail: orders@centralbooks.com
Website: www.centralbooks.co.uk

Contents

Author's acknowledgements

This book is the result of the collaborative work of the ESRC Research Group on Care, Values and the Future of Welfare (CAVA) based at the University of Leeds between 1999 and 2004. I am very grateful to Carol Smart, Simon Duncan and Bren Neale for access to the imaginative research on family lives and personal relationships they have produced over the years, and to them, Sasha Roseneil and Sarah Irwin for their helpful comments on different chapters. I would like to thank Harrie Churchill for her assistance with the first two chapters, Alan Deacon for his comments and responsiveness, and Jean Carabine, Joe Deacon and Rowan Deacon for their support. I owe particular thanks to Keleigh Groves who lived the book with me, and to Angela Phillips, CAVA's Media Fellow, who creatively reshaped parts of it. We are all grateful to the Economic and Social Research Council for funding the research, to Paula Ridley and the Calouste Gulbenkian Foundation for suggesting and funding the book, and to Felicity Luard for smoothing its production.

Fiona Williams

Preface

Few people of a certain age can forget the impact of *Family and Kinship in East London*, Michael Young and Peter Wilmott's masterly 1957 study of family patterns in the East End. In *Rethinking Families*, Fiona Williams and her colleagues show that today's families can be configured rather differently from the traditional mother/father/children and extended family of close relatives but perform the same functions of support and care. Today's families are likely to include step-fathers/step-mothers/step-siblings, or same-sex parents, and have extended families which do not necessarily involve blood ties but engage a wider circle of friends in the sustaining of young and old.

Williams argues that a diversity of living arrangements and family groups are increasingly the norm and should be recognised as such; in fact, the word 'families' is much preferred to 'family' as a way of describing these new groupings and how they work. There is no indication, however, that the traditional roles of nurture and care have been abandoned – they are simply carried out within different, and sometimes non-consanguineous and changing sets of relatives.

The idea of the traditional 'family' has a huge cultural resonance and is an ideal that has become embedded in aspiration as well as in reality. What do these changes mean for all of us – those attempting to make the traditional family work, those engaged in serial monogamy, as well as those making up their own individual families as they go along? Many countries prescribe rights and responsibilities according to legal definitions of relationships – what are the implications for policy-makers of this new world? In *Rethinking Families* Fiona Williams shows that, despite tensions between increasing independence from blood or marriage ties and the often complex accommodations that relationships now require, the ethic of care can express itself through a changing variety of family forms, and appears to be the most resilient cultural norm of all.

Paula Ridley
Director
Calouste Gulbenkian Foundation

Executive summary

The CAVA Research Programme on 'Care, Values and the Future of Welfare' at the University of Leeds is a five-year study funded by the Economic and Social Research Council into changes in parenting and partnering and the implications for future policy directions. That research is the basis of this book.

The context: chapters 1 and 2

Family lives are changing. Over our lifetimes many of us will cohabit, marry, separate, parent on our own, or do all of these. Our family support networks may well include parents and step-parents, children, close friends, same-sex partners, ex-partners or ex-sons- and daughters-in-law. There is greater acknowledgement of the diversity of living arrangements and family forms. Other social changes have altered the contours of family lives and personal relationships: more mothers work, we are an ageing society, more people live on their own, and global migration means that family commitments cross continents.

Public and academic debate about these changes tends to be polarised. On the one side, there are those who see in them a loss of commitment, a self-seeking individualism, a parenting deficit and a moral decline. Consumerism has, it is argued, fostered an individual acquisitiveness which has infected the domestic sphere. On the other side, changes in family lives and intimate relations are seen to herald the emergence of self-actualising men and women, less bound by obligation and duty, who have greater independence to pursue more satisfying and democratic relationships. Love acquires greater significance, yet its achievement becomes less certain. Chapter 1 sets out these changes and debates and argues that we need more empirical evidence about people's commitments and what it is that matters to them as their family lives and personal relationships change.

Policy reforms have responded to these changes by a move away from the 'male breadwinner' model of the old welfare state towards an 'adult worker' model in which paid work is a central principle of self-sufficiency and responsibility for men and women. However, this has set up some key tensions around work/life balance, women's and men's positions as carers and workers (since women are still the main carers and kin-keepers); whether we treat children as investments for the future or citizens of the present; and how far policy emphasises parenting support or parenting responsibility. In Chapter 2 we ask whether the new normative family that is emerging in policy matches the lived experience of people who are weighing up how to balance work, care, and commitments to family and friends.

The research findings: chapters 3 and 4

CAVA has developed five central research projects on aspects of family and relationship change: life after divorce; motherhood, work and care; non-conventional partnerships; transnational kinship; and collective groups and organisations who mobilise around parenting and partnering issues. The projects all used in-depth qualitative research methods (the methodology is explained in Appendix 2) and all were concerned to find out 'what matters' to people in the conditions of change in which they found themselves. When faced with new situations or dilemmas, we asked what influences them in working out the 'proper thing to do'?

The shape of commitments is changing but there is no loss of commitment. People are less dependent on blood or marriage ties; their commitments extend across different households linked by dissolved marriages, reconstituted families, non-resident partners and transnational kin. There may be more blurring of kin, ex-kin, sexual partners and friends in people's networks, but little of this indicates a loss of commitment itself. When faced with dilemmas they generally negotiate 'the proper thing to do' in and through their commitments to others, especially with reference to the well-being of their children. People may be finding new living arrangements; however, these are not simply individual lifestyle choices but ways of attending to the needs of, and their commitments to, close others. For example, we found that the living and re-partnering arrangements of divorced or separated parents could take the form of living without a partnership, having a partner who retains their own residence, or co-habiting with a new partner, as well as remarrying. Crucially, these 'choices' are about taking into account what is best for children, and which relationships, for example, with ex-partners or grandparents, are important to sustain.

Sex and living together are no longer essential bedfellows. Sex and marriage became uncoupled in the 1960s, marriage and parenthood followed in the 1980s, and now it is likely that many people will spend some time in their lives living alone or living with someone who is not their sexual partner. Indeed, generally, friends play a more important part in people's networks of support than has been recognised. It is perhaps a marker of the importance of these relationships in people's lives that, as we found, 'friendship' has become a key metaphor invoking the quality of a relationship marked by closeness, confiding, sharing and mutuality, whether with older children or with other kin.

People care in different ways. Perceptions of what it means to be a good mother or father are influenced by what is customary in local social networks. The research draws on data from the 2001 Census to map the geography of family formations and to show how the variability in the UK of working and caring patterns is subject to local cultural, economic and social contexts. Against this background, mothers (and fathers) arrive at different decisions about taking up paid employment when they have children. Some work part time, some full time, and some not at all. Whatever the outcome, central to these decisions for parents is what, in the circumstances, is the right thing for their child. This form of moral reasoning is at odds with assumptions that money alone determines whether parents will take up paid work.

When changes conflict with values. Some changes in family life conflict with deeply held beliefs about divorce, or marriage outside faith. People cope with this by weighing up how best to sustain their relationships with people who matter to them. Grandparents, for example, will provide much-needed financial and childcare support to divorced or separated children even though they disapprove of divorce in principle. Culture is not fixed, but dynamically reconstitutes itself.

When the support of friends and family is not enough. Self-help groups play an important role in communities in providing the sort of care and support that people say they want: that is, based on reciprocity, trust, mutual respect, informality and being non-judgemental. In addition, those involved develop their own forms of shared expertise about coping with adversity.

What, in the circumstances, is the proper thing to do? This is the question people ask themselves when faced with dilemmas. Whether they are talking about divorce, or whether to take on the care of a relative needing support, or how to have the baby cared for when they go back to work, what many people share is not an agreement on a set of abstract moral imperatives, but a moral and social weighing-up of the given situation. People negotiate within certain guidelines according to the context in which they find themselves. The question they ask is not so much 'What *ought* I to do?' but 'How can I best manage this?' Far from their being demoralised individuals, there is a palpable moral texture to people's lives. Moral reasoning based on *care* informs the way people attempt to balance their own sense of self with the needs of others. What it means to be a good mother, father, grandparent, partner, ex-partner, lover, son, daughter or friend is crucial to the way people negotiate the proper thing to do. As people work through their dilemmas, certain practical ethics emerge for adults and children, ethics which enable resilience, which facilitate commitment and which lie at the heart of people's interdependency. They include being attentive to others' situations, accommodating one's own needs to those of others, adapting to others' changing identities, and being non-judgemental and open to making and receiving reparation. Children also value fairness, respect, care, communication and trust in coping with changes in their family lives. Together these ethics constitute a form of compassionate realism which enables people to find ways of coping with changes in their family lives and personal relationships.

Our recommendations: chapter 5

Using the evidence from our research we propose that the significance that people place on care and commitment in their lives is underestimated by policy-makers in three ways. First, it is often assumed that contemporary social change means that people have lost their moral commitment or they are too self-interested to understand the meaning of commitment. Second, much of the caring activity that happens is taken for granted, made invisible and not valued. Third, policies are often based on an assumption that what impels people is the financial advantage that paid work brings, rather than the commitment they have to others. We argue that an ethic of care based on recognising the significance of people's care commitments, and the contribution these make to citizenship, would find greater support in developing policies than arguments based on the ethic of work alone. This involves:

Balancing the work ethic with the care ethic. We start with the question: how do we best support each other? We argue that the care ethic recognises that care is universal and that it emphasises interdependency, acknowledges vulnerability, and encourages trust and tolerance; these are important civic virtues that sustain social cohesion. Having time to care should be something that is expected by all citizens. Caring activity should be valued, respected and supported by both legislation and services.

Making time to care. This requires support for flexible working hours and conditions, access to affordable good-quality care provision, and a framework of financial support so that men and women can choose how best to combine paid work and care. It also requires better pay and conditions and training for care workers. To achieve all this will require innovative thinking and dialogue nationally and locally about the reorganisation of time and space in order to meet people's expectations of how to care properly for others, for themselves and for the communities in which they live.

Supporting parents and listening to them. State support needs to overcome mistrust and provide support that respects, is non-judgemental and practical, and gives its users a voice. Some groups remain relatively unsupported locally and nationally, especially minority ethnic families and families with a disabled adult or child. Support should be based on an understanding of the existing moral basis to people's commitments and sense of responsibility rather than on the conditions of 'no rights without responsibilities'.

Recognising that investment in care is for the present, not just the future.
Current policies for children are framed in terms of the contribution they will make
to society in the future. This is important, but we need to respect childhood and give
children a voice in the here-and-now too. A care ethic recognises that good-quality
care and support brings dividends for the present in terms of improved relationships,
creativity, sociability, emotional well-being and greater self-determination for both
carer and cared-for, be they children, older or disabled people.

Protecting diversity from inequalities. Policies based on the ethic of care should
recognise and value care, but must not reinforce differences and inequalities between
men and women or between different communities or localities. Policies need to be
diverse and flexible enough to meet people's varying options for their living arrangements and for combining work and care in the short term. They also have to be part
of a longer-term vision that attends to the complex inequalities and hierarchies that
are part of current caring practices between men and women, adults and children,
and carers and cared-for.

1

Figuring out the changes

If governments are to support the capacity of people to care for themselves and each other in ways they think fit, it is important to understand how people experience changes in family lives and personal relationships and what values inform their actions. We have called this book *Rethinking Families* because our work in this area leads us to believe that what is most urgent, whether we are talking about work/life balance, lives after divorce, civil partnerships, children and risk, the care deficit or the care workforce, is a new framework for thinking about families, relationships and care.

Over our lifetimes many of us will cohabit, marry, separate, parent on our own, or do all of these things. Our family support networks may well include parents and step-parents, children, close friends, ex-partners or ex-sons- and daughters-in-law. We have a greater diversity of living arrangements and family forms. As can be seen in Figures 1–4, overleaf, there is an increased incidence of cohabitation, separation, divorce, lone parenthood, step-families and people living on their own; and there is a greater acknowledgement of same-sex relationships.

Such changes in family form rest on, or interact with, other changes – economic, social, cultural and demographic – which impact upon family relations: women's participation in the labour market has increased; housing costs have risen; children are financially dependent on their parents for longer; there is less experience of lifelong marriage; a multicultural and global society makes for a diversity of family traditions and for care commitments which may stretch across continents. Women having fewer children, or having them later or not at all, along with an ageing society, have also served to alter the courses of our lives compared with previous generations (see Boxes 1 and 2, pages 14–15). And, as Table 1 on page 16 shows, Britain is not alone in experiencing such changes.

This chapter looks at the main contours of change in family lives and the debates that have accompanied these developments. Chapter 2 focuses on the changing policy context. Both draw attention to some of the gaps between ideas about what

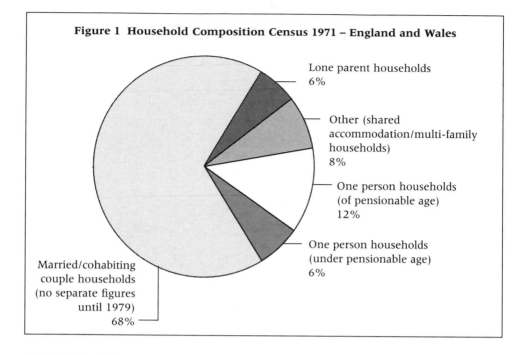

Figure 1 Household Composition Census 1971 – England and Wales

Lone parent households
6%

Other (shared accommodation/multi-family households)
8%

One person households (of pensionable age)
12%

One person households (under pensionable age)
6%

Married/cohabiting couple households (no separate figures until 1979)
68%

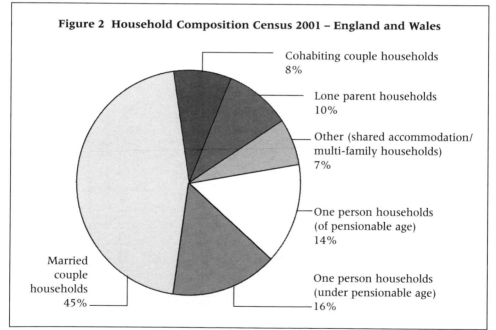

Figure 2 Household Composition Census 2001 – England and Wales

Cohabiting couple households
8%

Lone parent households
10%

Other (shared accommodation/ multi-family households)
7%

One person households (of pensionable age)
14%

One person households (under pensionable age)
16%

Married couple households
45%

Figures 1 and 2 represent the changes in living arrangements between 1971 and 2001. Over their lives individuals may belong to different categories. Between 1971 and 2001 the overall number of one person households, cohabiting couple households and lone parent households increased, while multi-family households – i.e. those comprising more than one family (one-third of lone parents lived in multi-family households in 1971) – and married couple families declined.

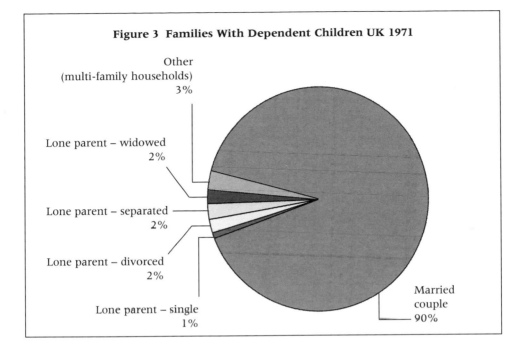

Figure 3 Families With Dependent Children UK 1971

Other
(multi-family households)
3%

Lone parent – widowed
2%

Lone parent – separated
2%

Lone parent – divorced
2%

Lone parent – single
1%

Married
couple
90%

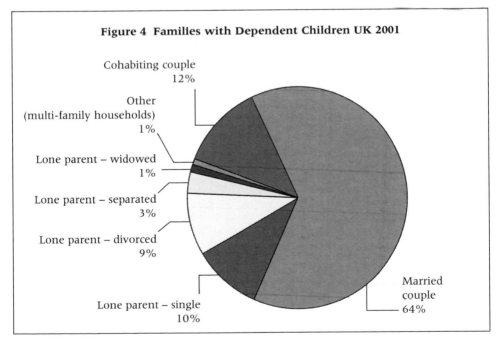

Figure 4 Families with Dependent Children UK 2001

Cohabiting couple
12%

Other
(multi-family households)
1%

Lone parent – widowed
1%

Lone parent – separated
3%

Lone parent – divorced
9%

Lone parent – single
10%

Married
couple
64%

Figures 3 and 4 represent the changes in family forms, showing a reduction in families headed by a married couple and in widowed lone parents, and an increase in the number of families headed by a separated, divorced or single lone parent and in cohabiting couples. Again, there is now more frequent movement between these family forms in the course of an individual's life.

Box 1 A Picture of Parenting and Partnering in the 2000s[1]

- *On average families have 1.6 children;*
- *Around 40% of children experience parental divorce by their 16th birthday;*
- *Around 40% of births occur outside of marriage;*
- *8% of lone parent families were headed by a lone father in 2001;*
- *43% of women and 37% of men aged 20–35 cohabited in 2001;*
- *70% of marriages are preceded by a period of cohabitation;*
- *21% of dependent children live in poverty, a third of these in lone mother families;*
- *55% of families with disabled children live in poverty;*
- *Minority ethnic groups make up 8% of the UK population and 10% of the under-16 population;*
- *65% of women aged 16–59 with dependent children were in employment in 2001; 26% worked full time and 39% worked part time;*
- *70% of fathers work over 40 hours a week and 14% work over 60 hours a week;*
- *Women on average earn 19% less a week than men in comparable employment;*
- *17% of couple families have a sole male breadwinner;*
- *30% of grandmothers and 25% of grandfathers saw their eldest grandchild once a week in 1999;*
- *Women spend 1 hour 30 minutes more than men doing housework, cooking, cleaning and ironing on a weekday;*
- *14% of women and 11% of men over 16 provided informal care for relatives and friends in 2001;*
- *56% of men and 37% of women aged 20–24 lived with their parents in 2003.*

Families in the 2000s are characterised by diversity, continuity and change. There is a diversity of living arrangements for partnering and parenting although the majority of families with children are headed by a couple. Families are changing, with more parental separation, smaller families and more working mothers. However, a significant percentage of children continue to live in poverty.

'the family' *should* look like and what family lives *do* look like. In order to explore what actually goes on in family lives and personal relationships, Chapters 3 and 4 focus in greater detail on the different ways in which adults and children cope with what are often new situations in their lives, such as divorce, separation, remarriage, step-families, combining work and care, living alone or caring across continents. Drawing on this research, we address in Chapter 5 questions of how to support care and commitments in close personal and family relationships. We develop ideas for a political 'ethic of care' to assist policy-makers, practitioners and voluntary organisa-tions, as well as other researchers, as they think through their policies and priorities.

Box 2 Key Changes over the last 30 years[2]

- *Divorce rates have doubled;*
- *Cohabitation has trebled;*
- *The proportion of children living with a lone parent or with cohabiting parents has doubled;*
- *Single person households have doubled;*
- *Average family size has decreased from 2.9 children to 1.6 children;*
- *Five times as many babies are born outside of marriage;*
- *The proportion of the population aged under 16 has decreased from 24% to 20% while the proportion of the population aged over 60 has increased from 16% to 21%;*
- *The full-time employment rate of women with dependent children has trebled and their part-time employment rate has doubled;*
- *The number of students in further and higher education has trebled;*
- *The average age when women have their first child has increased by 5 years;*
- *The proportion of childless women aged over 25 has increased 25% since 1975;*
- *The employment rate of males has dropped by 14%;*
- *Parents report spending three times as much time with their children per day.*

As well as indicating increases in cohabitation, divorce and lone parent and single person households, these figures show the extension of dependency of children on their parents and the increased importance of a female wage for household resources. Note, however, since 2000 there has been a slight downward trend in divorce.

Who and what are 'families'?

> *'Every family has a secret and the secret is that it is not like other families. If only people knew what we were really like, my mother thought – her not getting up until ten in the morning and none of us sitting down to a proper breakfast – they'd have nothing to do with us. We pretend we're normal but it's only a matter of time before folks find out what we're like.'* Alan Bennett recalls his childhood in the 1940s and 50s.[3]

Academic research often mirrors social change and this is true for studies of family and kinship.[4] Studies in the 1950s, 60s and 70s such as those by Young and Willmott focused upon the structure and function of families and showed how far the nuclear family, as a social institution, had adapted to meet the demands of modern society, or how kinship networks operated in local communities.[5] More recently, research has been framed by a notion of *family practices*: what we do rather than what we are.[6]

Table 1 European Comparisons[7]

	UK	France	Germany	Sweden	Spain	Netherlands
Fertility rate (average number of births per woman aged 15–49)	1.7	1.9	1.4	1.5	1.2	1.7
Divorce rate (divorces per 100 marriages)	53	41	44	54	17	39
Births outside marriage (% of all births)	41	44	25	56	18	29
Age at first birth (average for female population aged 15–44)	30	30	29	28	29	29
Single person households (%)	29	31	36	47	17	33
Children living in in households 60% below mean income, after housing costs (% of children)	30	24	24	10	25	13
% of children in lone parent families	21	17	21	23	3	13
Employment rate women:men (% of female/male adult population)	70:80	56:70	59:72	73:76	44:73	67:83
Average working hours for women (full time: part time)	39:18	38:23	40:18	39:23	41:18	39:19
Average working hours for men (full time: part time)	44:18	40:23	42:16	39:19	43:19	41:19

Many of these changes are occurring across European countries. However, the UK has a higher divorce rate, more lone parent households, higher rates of child poverty and longer working hours for men. The figures here are for 2000 and 2001.

The concept of family practices focuses on the everyday interactions with close and loved ones and moves away from the fixed boundaries of co-residence, marriage, ethnicity and obligation that once defined the white, heterosexual, male breadwinner nuclear family. It registers the ways in which our networks of affection are not simply given by virtue of blood or marriage but are negotiated and shaped by us, over time and place. These networks are, of course, influenced by wider forces such as employment, globalisation, social norms, and views of what is right and proper. However, in weighing up how we behave towards those we love and care for, in the circumstances in which we find ourselves (How do I balance time for myself with time for my partner? How will divorce affect my children's relationship with their paternal grandmother?), we also contribute to the reshaping of social norms. Family practices are fluid: they are responsive to and productive of change.

Intimacy and partnerships

An understanding of how close personal relationships have changed – the *transformation of intimacy* as Anthony Giddens calls it[8] – has also hastened the move away from examining the structures and obligations of family life. The study of intimate partnerships has provided a new lens to help us understand how there are greater expectations in the *quality* of personal relationships and that this quality has to be achieved; it cannot be assumed just because a couple have agreed to be together. This emphasis on quality characterises what Giddens calls the 'pure relationship', freed from traditional forms of duty and obligation. Communication and negotiation become central to this achievement, and success cannot be guaranteed. There is thus an uncertainty about intimate relationships; they are contingent upon their capacity to meet mutual expectations. These new notions of intimacy have made possible a greater inclusiveness in the study of family practices, for example in giving recognition to gay and lesbian relationships, step-families, and close friendships.[9]

Caring and kin-keeping

However, while a focus on intimacy can reveal more about the close relationships between adults, it tends to underplay the importance of relationships between children and their parents, or commitments to other kin and friends.

All these relationships involve *caring activity*. Research into care and caring practices, which we describe later, has revealed the important dimensions of day-to-day activities which are so central to the sustaining of family lives and personal relationships – helping, tending, looking out for, thinking about, talking, sharing, and offering a shoulder to cry on. This research has made visible the ways in which, in the main, women are the carers and 'kin-keepers'.[10] But these activities are not simple obligations – they are negotiated according to what people think is 'the proper thing to do' in terms of who they are and the context that they are in. People develop their webs of commitment over time and these can transcend ties of blood, marriage, sex and friendship and, in a globalised world, cross cultures and continents.

We all need care, but an understanding of care is incomplete without a perspective on those who chiefly 'receive' it – children and disabled and older people. The disabled people's movement has challenged the notion that they are or should be considered the objects of others' care.[11] Research on childhood has repositioned children as moral actors in their own and their families' lives, rather than as passive objects of concern or remedy.[12]

Re-imagining the family

This account of developments in academic research begins to indicate some of the ways in which family lives and personal relationships have changed – from the nuclear family, where men, women and children knew their place, to diverse family forms with increasingly fluid and negotiated relationships. The external moral codes of religion or state now hold less of a grip on the partnering and parenting practices of many. The separation of sex from marriage, so hotly debated in the 1960s, has been followed by the loosening of marriage from parenthood. Women have assumed the right – or responsibility – to be earners (Boxes 1 and 2, pages 14–15, show the increase in women's participation in the labour market). But here we need to strike a note of caution and introduce a further distinction in order to make sense of family lives. The nuclear family of the post-war world, with its male breadwinner, was a construction of what family life *should* look like. There *were* single parents in the 1950s (many were war widows, and more never-married lone mothers lived with their parents then than do now; see Figures 1 and 2, page 12), and there were also working mothers, and same-sex relationships, but these did not fit the normative picture of family life.

We need to distinguish between, on the one hand, the *normative family* and, on the other, the *lived experiences* of family lives and personal relationships, and see how each influences the other. It is through government policies, the law, professional practices, research, the media, television soaps and sitcoms, that the normative family enters the public imagination.

But it is not simply that a normative or idealised model of family life is constructed for us. John Gillis, the American historian of family life, has documented the ways in which we all construct imagined family lives that we live *by* (in contrast to the actual ones we live *with*). For example, in their hurried and harried lives, those who can afford it may have a holiday cottage or caravan, a rural retreat of ordered and aesthetic tranquillity, where they seek to protect the integrity of their family life, so that 'it is at a distance that families come to know themselves'.[13] Television home makeover programmes similarly appeal to our imagined domestic lives. We develop new rituals and refashion old ones to act out the symbolic importance of our close ties, and these provide a trail that links past to present to future. The graduation ceremony, once in the 1960s and 70s an optional extra, has now become a ritual that makes educational achievement the symbolic marker not only of adult independence, but of mutual love, support and ongoing commitment between parents and their children. Beyond kin, the school reunion has become an occasion which gives some sense of continuity in an uncertain world.

One question we pursue in this book is whether a new normative family is taking shape, and how far this fits with people's lived experiences. Are we moving away from the old male breadwinner model towards a dual male-and-female worker model, and what does that hold for us? Are there new expectations around parental or partner responsibilities and do these fit with lived experiences? Are we moving towards more democratic family relationships? In other words, while the normative family of policy prescription might deviate from our lived experience, there may too be a divergence between our own practices and our sense of what intimate relationships and/or parenthood should be about. A couple may believe in fair sharing of household tasks but in practice things may end up differently, for all sorts of reasons.

Interpreting family and relationship change

The movement away from the prescribed gender, sexual, and work roles of the past is the subject of much social debate, social theory and considerable anxiety. Two main interpretations dominate the literature, the pessimistic and the optimistic. There is, in addition, a third perspective which questions both.

The pessimists' demoralisation thesis

Here, increased divorce and cohabitation, more children born outside marriage and more lone parenting are seen to represent moral decline, and to bring with them harmful effects.[14] Children are damaged, socially, emotionally and educationally, by divorce, and go on to repeat the pattern with their own children. Cohabitation is seen as a flight from commitment, liable to produce welfare dependency and unstable unions which are bad for children (cohabitations involving children are less likely to lead to marriage and last on average less than two years). The children of lone parents lack a father figure and a male wage, which makes them, especially boys, vulnerable to inadequate parenting and poverty.[15] For some commentators, crime is directly linked to this. Absent fathers who renege on, or are not able to accept, their responsibilities as providers for their families are assumed to lack commitment and moral purpose. The decline of the male breadwinner, the rise of women's financial and social independence, and the acceptance of a diversity of sexual lifestyles (all shown in Box 2) have contributed to a moral vacuum in relation to the family. This loss of the 'family values' of duty, fidelity and responsibility has been replaced by self-ish individualism, an unfulfilled quest for personal autonomy, and more generalised social instability. One response to this situation is to retrieve marriage from the arena of private choice and to treat it as a social good which deserves public policy support and encouragement on the basis that 'Families based on marriage are, on average, healthier, wealthier and more stable than other family forms'.[16]

Such arguments are often associated with right-wing neo-conservative traditional-ists. However, one variation, from a socialist perspective, connects this rise of selfish individualism and hollowing out of moral values to developments in capitalism. De-industrialisation is here seen to have undermined men's breadwinning capacity and led to the break-up of families and of the stable working-class communities in which they thrived.[17] Contemporary capitalism has corroded moral character, and destroyed virtues such as trust and cohesion. Consumerism fosters an acquisitive individualism which has infected the private sphere. Individual choice and pleasure have become the rationale for the pursuit of private relationships. All this is bad news for love, care and commitment.[18]

A communitarian variation on this theme identifies a 'parenting deficit', meaning that in the movement of both parents into work, the values of careerism and consumption have weakened commitment to care for children.[19] This has precipitated crime, anti-social behaviour and mental illness. Women – the former guardians of care – are becoming like men. The solution is to balance the economic right to work with a heightened moral sense of responsibility to others, especially children, with flexitime at work, stay-at-home allowances, inducements to marry and disincentives to divorce.

The optimists' democratisation thesis

In spectacular contrast, other social theorists have seen the move away from traditional gender divisions, assumptions of lifelong marriage, duty and dependence as heralding relationships that are more equal and mutually satisfying, because they are no longer held in place by obligation and convention, but are negotiated.[20] The key process of change which is central to this thesis is that of *individualisation*. This is not the same as individualism, but rather refers to the way in which individuals, once freed from old constraints and conventions, can begin to shape their own biographies and identities and reflect on the meaning of their relationships. For women, in particular, access to a wage unlocks their dependency on men. Unlike selfish individualism, the spur for people's individualised relationships is to find ways to sustain mutual respect, happiness and satisfaction. Ultimately, these relationships contribute to the democratisation of both gender relations and the family, as each member is seen as an individual in their own right.

The pursuit of satisfaction is not without difficulty and some see the effort to shape one's own life as giving rise to a greater need for affinity with a close other. Love acquires greater not less significance, yet its achievement becomes more uncertain. Some argue that this uncertainty has meant that parent–child relationships have replaced marriage and adult partnerships as the new lifelong emotional investment.[21] Partners come and go but the parent–child relationship goes on forever. Figure 5, opposite, shows the findings of a survey asking parents in their twenties and thirties what gave them most happiness. A noticeably higher rating is given to 'my children' than to 'my relationship', by both men and women.

Gay and lesbian partnerships and families are seen as pioneers in this quest to make personal relationships more egalitarian. This is because they enjoy relative freedom from the gendered conventions that encompass heterosexual relationships.[22] Other non-traditional but close caring relationships, such as those based on friendship, or those where partners are not co-resident, have similarly been identified as trailblazers in attempting to find alternative ways of dealing with the tension, inherent in many co-resident sexual relationships, of balancing autonomy with connectedness.[23]

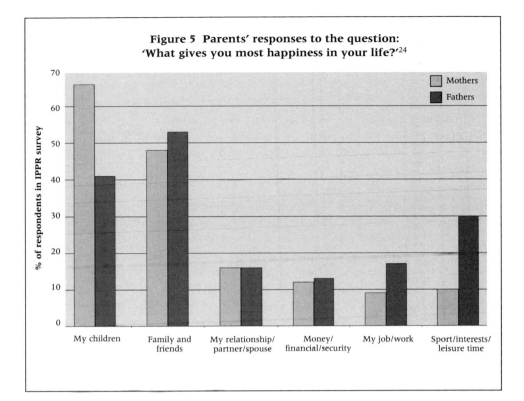

Figure 5 Parents' responses to the question: 'What gives you most happiness in your life?'[24]

A concern for complexity: continuity and change

Another perspective argues that diversity was a feature of families in the past: for example, the eighteenth-century household contained members who were connected by friendship as well as those connected by blood or marriage, and all were considered 'family'.[25] External moral codes may have placed sex firmly within marriage in the early twentieth century, but this simply generated ways of hiding illegitimacy rather than abolishing it. Both the pessimistic and optimistic views can be challenged on the grounds that they overstate their case and that, where the optimists underestimate old practices inside new forms, the pessimists fail to spot continuing processes in the decline of old family forms.[26]

The study in 1980 by Wallerstein and Kelly of 60 American families on and after divorce contributed, at the time, to the 'demoralisation' view that divorce led to bad parenting and was harmful to children.[27] But the study also shows how easy it is to overstate the extent of change and to underestimate the uneven consequences of some of the more dramatic statistics. In fact, it is possible to read their findings through a different lens: this shows that for every post-divorce family they interviewed whose children had later problems, there were as many whose children were flourishing.[28] One of the key factors was the quality of the parenting before the divorce, and particularly whether the children were treated with respect, and whether their views were listened to and recognised. It was therefore important not to assume that divorce causes a particular effect, but to understand the *processes* through which some adults and children were better able to negotiate change than others.

What many broad-brush theories of the pessimists and the optimists fail to capture is the variability of different groups' experience of change. For example, the increase in lone parents is seen as a marked feature of change in household form. Recent policies for lone mothers have regarded their growing numbers with alarm and focused on getting them 'off welfare and into work', as lone parenting has been equated with 'welfare dependency'. However, this picture can be misleading. Lone parenting is not new and does not inevitably mean 'welfare dependency'. Not only has lone parenting been a consistent feature of African-Caribbean women's lives in Britain for the last 50 years, but African-Caribbean single mothers have a high rate of economic activity, with around 57% in paid work.[29] On the other hand, less than 10% of Pakistani and Bangladeshi households are headed by a single parent.[30] These statistics point to ethnic variations which tend to be ignored by generalising theories. Ethnic variations can also co-exist with common trends for minority ethnic groups. For example, all black and South Asian groups are more likely than the white population to be in poverty; almost two-thirds of Pakistani and Bangladeshi households are poor.[31]

The democratisation thesis also tends to underestimate the extent to which considerable (old) gender inequalities continue to exist in (new) couple relationships. Most obvious is the persistence of domestic violence: one in four women will experience it at some point in their lives.[32] In relation to housework and the care of children, women do twice as much as men, whether they work outside the home or not (see Box 1, page 14). This can lead some women to place a premium on the practical involvement of their partner rather than on the capacity to negotiate and communicate.[33] Similarly, it is easy to overstate the democratisation of the parent–child relationship through talk and communication, for much depends on the relations of power between adults and children. For some young people, autonomy is maintained by *not* disclosing all feelings, especially where disclosure is one-sided.[34] Respect for that privacy is more important than negotiated communication, in some situations. In addition, material factors can disrupt egalitarian ideals. Women's involvement in paid work has not resulted in wholesale economic independence: low wages, part-time work and lack of affordable child- and eldercare support for working mothers see to that (see Box 1). In fact, it is this *unevenness* of change, where old practices jostle with new ideals of equality between men and women which, some say, gives rise to the necessity for continual negotiation between couples or between parents and children.[35]

The democratisation thesis seems to imply that there is a timeline from fixed traditional to individualised modern relationships along which men and women and their children will inexorably travel. However, people's responses to change are complex, and are rooted in an interaction between beliefs, the context in which they find themselves, and their commitment to others. Some Pakistani and Bangladeshi families believe that arranged marriages are the best way to continue their commitments to kin in their countries of origin, but at the same time may also have high educational aspirations for both their sons and their daughters.[36] Change does not happen in a straightforward way. Take the case of mothers and fathers' sharing work and childcare as an example of democratisation: a study comparing survey data from parents who were 33 years old in 1991 with data from parents who were 30 in 2000 shows that mothers of the younger cohort report slightly *less* involvement of fathers in childcare in 2000 than did their counterparts in 1991. This survey reports a 'stalling' of moves to more egalitarian arrangements. Also, despite the popular view of 'new dads' being a middle-class phenomenon, fathers with fewer educational qualifications are reported to help out *more* with childcare than professional fathers.[37]

The persistence of inequalities *between* families is another important aspect of continuity glossed over by the democratisation thesis. Families in which both partners have educational qualifications have been better placed to withstand the increased costs of housing because they can command wages high enough to cover the cost of childcare. It also means they are able to offer their children more financial help with their education and accommodation costs. These dynamics have contributed to the widening gap between what are called work-rich (but time-poor) households, and unemployed, or work-poor, households.[38] Families continue to be vectors of advantage and disadvantage.

Conclusion

Generalising theories, or even aggregate statistics, cannot fully capture the variability, processes and meanings in people's responses to change. That part of the picture requires a closer investigation of people's own experiences. Rather than assuming that the lessening of influence of a morality 'from above' has resulted in moral abandonment, we need to know *what does matter and seems proper* to those parents who find themselves in situations such as divorce, or cohabitation, for which there appears to be no clear script to guide their actions. What kinds of commitment are important in the circumstances they find themselves? What matters to parents who attempt to combine work and care? What is the image that people have of their relationships, and what do they actually do? And how does all this relate to the normative family that is constructed through policy and law?

The next chapter looks at this policy context, for it too has been changing. The 'normative family' of the post-war world – the lifelong-married nuclear family with the man as breadwinner – is no longer the one which has emerged out of the development of family law and policy since the 1970s.

Summary

- There have been significant changes in the contours of family lives and personal relationships over the last 30 years with increased cohabitation, separation, divorce, lone parenthood, more step-families and people living on their own, and greater acknowledgement of same-sex relationships.

- These have been accompanied by other social changes – increases in mothers' employment, an ageing society, a multicultural society and widening inequalities.

- Research on family lives and personal relationships has moved away from looking at the family as a social institution. Three concepts inform the study of family lives and personal relationships: *family practices, intimacy* and *care*.

- It is important to distinguish between the normative family (what the family *should* look like) and the lived experiences of individuals.

- Two main interpretations of family change dominate public and academic debates. On the one side, the *pessimists* see changes in family life as bringing moral decline, a lack of social stability and solidarity, a parenting deficit and selfish individualism. On the other, the *optimists* identify a process of individualisation whereby people are relieved of fixed conventions and constraints and can begin to shape their lives and relationships. This makes possible the pursuit of more open, democratic and mutually rewarding relationships but it also means that as love acquires greater not less significance, its achievement becomes more uncertain.

- Empirical evidence of changes in families and personal relations leads towards a more cautious approach to claims that society is collapsing or that close relationships are being democratised. The old exists in the new and the new in the old; empirical research indicates significant unevenness and variability in the way people experience and cope with change. There are also continuing economic inequalities between families.

NOTES

1   Broomfield (2004); Dex (2003); Ermisch and
     Francesconi (2000); DWP (2003); ONS
     (2001a, 2003a, 2003b, 2003c, 2004b, 2004c,
     2004e); poverty is measured as household
     income below 60% of the mean average
     household income before housing costs.
2   Ferri, Bynner and Wadsworth (2003); ONS
     (2001b, 2003c, 2004b, 2004c, 2004d,
     2004e).
3   Bennett (2000), p. 38.
4   See Gittins (1993).
5   Parsons (1971); Young and Willmott (1957);
     Willmott and Young (1973).
6   Morgan (1996); Silva and Smart, eds (1999).
7   Eurostat (2004a, 2004b). Child poverty
     figures from Bradshaw (2002); OECD
     (2002); Martin and Kats (2003).
8   Giddens (1992); Jamieson (1998).
9   Plummer (1995); Weeks, Heaphy and
     Donovan (2001); Pahl and Spencer (2004);
     Roseneil and Budgeon (2004).
10   Finch and Mason (1993).
11   Oliver and Barnes (1998); Morris (1991).
12   Smart, Neale and Wade (2001); Alanen and
     Mayall (2001); Dahlberg, Moss and Pence
     (1999); James and Prout, eds (1997).
13   Gillis (2003), p. 5.
14   See Murray (1990); Morgan (1995, 2000);
     and Wilson (2003). A more specific
     argument (the 'new home economics')
     that sees women's earning power outside
     marriage as upsetting the cost–benefit
     equilibrium of the male earner/women carer
     family is forwarded by Becker (1986, 1991).
15   Cockett and Tripp's (1994) study of
     outcomes from divorce concluded that
     separated families experience greater
     hardship, unhappiness, truancy and
     mental health problems.

16   O'Neill (2003), p. 3.
17   Dennis and Erdos (1993).
18   See Sennett (1999) on capitalism, Fevre
     (2000) on the decline in moral sentiment,
     and Bauman (2003).
19   Etzioni (1993).
20   Giddens (1991, 1992, 1999); Beck and
     Beck-Gernsheim (1995, 2002).
21   Beck and Beck-Gernsheim (1995, 2002).
22   Stacey (1996); Weeks *et al.* (2001).
23   Roseneil and Budgeon (2004); Levin (2004);
     Heath (2004).
24   Source: IPPR (2004), p. 11.
25   Tadmoor (2001).
26   See for critiques: Jamieson (1998); Ribbens-
     McCarthy and Edwards, in Carling, Duncan
     and Edwards, eds (2002); Thompson and
     Holland (2002).
27   Wallerstein and Kelly (1980).
28   Neale and Smart (2001); Smart, ed. (2003);
     Hetherington (2003); Kelly (2003).
29   Duncan and Edwards (1999), p. 5; Reynolds,
     in Carling, Duncan and Edwards, eds (2002)
     notes that the economic activity rate is
     lower for the under-25s for African-
     Caribbean lone mothers.
30   ONS (2004a).
31   Defined as less than 60% of median income
     before housing costs – ONS (2001a).
32   Home Office (2000).
33   Jamieson (1998).
34   Neale and Smart (2001).
35   Lewis (2001b).
36   Modood, Beishon and Virdee (1994).
37   See Chapter 5 in Ferri, Bynner and
     Wadsworth, eds (2003).
38   See Chapters 4 and 6 in Ferri, Bynner and
     Wadsworth, eds (2003).

2

The policies and politics of changing families

Policies and laws are important in shaping family and personal relationships both in terms of the assumptions they make about normative family life – the proper way to be or 'do' family – but also in the resources they provide to improve people's well-being. This chapter traces recent developments in law and policy affecting family lives and personal relationships.[1] Appendix 1 provides a chronological chart of relevant policies.

Policy changes

Some of the most noticeable changes in family forms have happened over the last 20 years, and in that time it has been possible to see four shifts in the way policies have reshaped an understanding of marriage and family relations.

1   There has been a move in economic and welfare policy away from the 'male breadwinner' family towards an 'adult worker' model where both men and women are earners.
2   Marriage, partnerships, separation and divorce have become more of a private matter to be sorted out between the adults involved and are less subject to a morality 'from above'. Marriage and parenthood are no longer seen as inevitably belonging together.
3   Parenthood and parenting have become less a private matter and much more an issue of public regulation in ensuring parental responsibilities, in which the welfare of the child is the central moral and social concern.
4   There is increased recognition for previously excluded parents or partners: in particular, same-sex partnerships.

Each of these shifts carries with it sets of assumptions about what family lives and personal relationships should be. On the face of it, they appear to reflect what has been happening – women are working more, people may become parents whether they are married, cohabiting, divorced, unmarried and single, gay or lesbian, and parents are more focused on their children. So is the normative family in state policy similar to the family lives and personal relationships that we are part of? It is through this question of the tensions between the prescriptions of family policies and the realities in family lives and personal relationships that we look at the policies and politics of changing families and personal relationships. This discussion forms the basis of a series of empirical and policy questions which are taken up in Chapters 3, 4 and 5.

Changing the balance of work and care

The post-war welfare state was established in the 1940s on the assumption that men went out to work and women stayed at home. Both the system of work and the system of benefits depended on this 'male breadwinner' model. However, the model came under pressure to change in the 1960s, 70s and 80s, particularly from social movements such as the Women's Movement.[2] This was important in putting gender equality at work and childcare on the agenda, as well as bringing out into the open issues such as domestic violence and sexual abuse. However, by the 1990s, it had become apparent that the idealised picture of male provider and female carer no longer captured the reality of people's lives. There were:

- more women in the labour market;
- rises in divorce/separation, re-partnering, and lone parenthood;
- a decline in the manufacturing and old industries which had supplied men with jobs;
- a decline in public housing and an expectation of owner-occupation and increases in housing costs;
- an ageing population (with associated pension, health and care needs) and widening inequalities.

European responses

In response to similar pressures, welfare systems in many other parts of Europe have been redesigned on the basis of an adult worker model, where men and women expect, and are expected, to be paid workers. Women, under this model, should rely on the labour market rather than (or as well as) on their partners or the state to provide for their needs, their children's needs, their future pensions, and so on. Within the European Union, encouraging women into self-sufficiency through employment is a central plank of policy.

These same processes have also given rise to what in Europe is called the 'care deficit'. If women are working, European policy-makers have been asking, who will provide the child- and eldercare, and who will pay for it? How can work and life be better balanced for working people and their families? Welfare states in Europe have had different histories of combining work and care and have therefore responded differently to these pressures.[3] In France and Finland, where public childcare services are long established, there have been moves towards paying carers cash benefits or tax credits to stay at home, to employ someone to look after the child in the home, or to pay for other childcare provision. In Spain and Italy there has been a reliance on migrant workers to take up low-paid care work in the home.[4] The Netherlands has introduced a 'combination model' (that is, one combining work and care). This consists of labour market strategies to upgrade the value of part-time work by giving it the same entitlements as full-time work. This policy has been combined with provisions for working parents to allow both mothers and fathers to work part time and to use their non-working time to share care and domestic work in the home.

Sweden's policies for gender equity date back to the 1960s, with publicly subsidised high-quality child- and eldercare, generously paid parental leave arrangements and the right to a shorter working day. Although economic recession in the early 1990s reduced public spending in these areas, Sweden's most innovative policy since then has been to encourage men and women to share their childcare – fathers are entitled to take two months' paid leave and 50% of fathers do so.[5] In contrast, the approach in the UK has centred less on gender equity and more on policy and provisions to encourage men and women into the labour market.

Turning adults into workers

At the centre of New Labour's welfare reforms is the attempt to 'make work pay', that is, to use encouragement into the labour market as a way to tackle poverty, to provide support for lone parents and their children, and to improve productivity and global competitiveness. The New Deal has targeted the young unemployed and lone parents with support to get them into paid work. The ethic of work provides the financial rationale to get people 'off welfare and into work', and the moral imperative to turn people into better citizens. It is presented as:

- the route out of dependency into independence, economic self-sufficiency and self-provisioning (for example, of pensions);
- the solution to poverty and social exclusion;
- the role model to offer children (for both mothers and fathers);
- the glue that binds society together;
- the condition of eligibility to a range of benefits.

New Labour has also introduced support for people on low incomes and working parents to help to 'make work pay':

- Working Tax Credit helps low earners;
- Child Tax Credit gives tax relief for children;
- Childcare Tax Credit helps with childcare costs.

In addition, the National Childcare Strategy increased the number of childcare places by 350,000 between 1998 and 2003.[6] Some of these have been through Sure Start and Childcare Centres in poorer areas. Partly under pressure from European Union directives, the government has also introduced extended maternity leave and pay, paid paternity leave, enhanced rights for part-time workers, unpaid time off for dependants in emergencies and rights for workers with young children to ask employers if they can work part time. In this picture parents are positioned primarily as 'partners' with the state and the voluntary and business sectors, vested with the responsibility of ensuring that their children behave responsibly and are sufficiently informed and educated to become citizen-workers themselves. Nevertheless, such measures are unprecedented in Britain, where for the most part childcare for working parents has been seen as something parents will sort out for themselves.

Carers at work

The gap between the normative adult worker model and people's lived experiences is largely caused by the constraints on women's capacity to become financially self-sufficient. To begin with, women's relationship to paid work is more complex than men's because (whether full- or part-time workers) they still take the major responsibility for childcare and work in the home. At the same time, full-time work is still, on the whole, organised around a male working model – nine to five and a linear career pattern. In some industries, such as banking, hours and conditions have become more demanding. Women with young children tend to be in part-time work, the biggest increases in female full-time employment being amongst women with higher educational qualifications whose partners are also employed. There are still disparities between women and men workers, women earning on average 82% of a male wage,[7] and much part-time work is casual and low-paid. Lower earnings restrict women's potential to save for a pension, with the result that single and divorced women are particularly vulnerable to poverty in older age.

Care while we work

Research suggests that a majority of mothers prefer to use informal carers such as grandparents or partners for their children under five – and payment of these is not allowed with the Childcare Tax Credit.[8] Most childcare provision is in the private sector, and in spite of financial help, for those not on professional salaries is just too expensive – childcare costs are 25% of the average household income.[9] This may be why only 13% of those eligible to receive financial support for childcare had taken up their Childcare Tax Credits in 2002.[10] Getting people into work, rather than valuing their care responsibilities, has been the rationale for these reforms. So it is perhaps not surprising that what working parents complain about most is not having enough time to spend with their children and work not offering them the flexibility to manage care and home responsibilities.[11] The low value given to care is reflected in the poor wages paid to people who work in care services and the low priority many employers give to people's care commitments.[12] In the work/life balance, work continues to weigh more heavily.

Given these hurdles the majority of women with children do not earn enough to be self-sufficient. It is more accurate to say that there exists in Britain, not an adult worker model, but a variety of patterns of combining work and care, with the 'one-and-a-half-earner' household being common.[13] In addition, the move to acknowledge men and women as independent earners is not recognised in social security where the new tax credit measures still regard the couple and not the individual as the basic unit of assessment. Nevertheless, if a dual-worker norm is emerging, we need to know how people experience this. What matters to them in combining work and family life? After all, mothers with young children are often facing a new situation for which there are no set rules. What influences the decisions they make? Is the adult worker model what people aspire to? And are there other models that could help? We look at these questions in Chapters 4 and 5.

From marriage to parenting

If rises in divorce rates and in the number of lone parents threatened the male breadwinner family then they also, along with the increases in cohabitation and the greater visibility of same-sex relationships, appeared to signal the end of lifelong heterosexual marriage as the normal life-pattern. People have not gone off marriage altogether – 40% of marriages are remarriages[14] – but one of the major shifts in family law in the 1970s was to see marriage and divorce as issues of a couple's own making and unmaking, rather than subject to the 'higher' moral code of the church and the state. In doing this, law and policy (the Divorce Reform Act, 1969, the Family Law Reform Act of 1987, and the Children Act of 1989 – see Appendix 1) also uncoupled marriage from parenthood. That is to say, what came under scrutiny was not the relationship between *husbands and wives* (whether one had behaved more badly than the other or whether they were married), but their responsibilities as *mothers and fathers* (and therefore the welfare of their children). The message these shifts in policy carried was that marriages or cohabitations may break up, but parents' responsibilities for their children continue. At first sight, policy would seem to reflect people's practice. Nevertheless, a number of twists in the story reveal key tensions in how we understand marriage, divorce, partnerships, parenting and the place of children.

From spouses to parents

In the 1969 Divorce Reform Act concern for the innocence or guilt of separating partners was to some extent set aside in favour of adequate provision for the children. Over time divorce became less a matter concerning husbands and wives than one between fathers and mothers. By the 1980s, divorce practices tended to follow a 'clean break' approach, where financial obligations would be settled at divorce. Underlying this was an idea that ex-wives could look after themselves either through paid work, or more usually through remarriage. However, while that law marked a process of retreat from state intervention in moral matters, leaving it instead to men and women to sort out their affairs on divorce (with the help of solicitors and the courts), it was accompanied by more intense pressure on fathers in other areas.

The attempt to make 'absent fathers' liable for the costs of their children was the aim of the 1981 Child Support Act. This was a response to moral outrage at stories of irresponsible men who fathered children only to leave them, and to a concern that single and divorced mothers were becoming dependent on the state for support. It was also attempting to reinstate men as breadwinners, and one of the ways it did this was to emphasise their role as *fathers*.

The Children Act of 1989 established that even when parents divorced or separated, their responsibilities to their children remained. It thus took the final step towards seeing the responsibilities of divorcing couples less as spouses and more as mothers and fathers. Whereas the state developed a lighter touch in the moral ordering of spouses, it became more heavily involved in the regulation of parents. The Act was important in that it focused attention upon the *quality* of parent–child relationships rather than simply on what the law required of parents. Parenthood began to be seen as something parents *do* rather than something they *are*. This was reflected later in the public education campaigns against domestic violence.[15]

Parents and the state

Parental responsibility was further reinforced in the 1990s by New Labour's introduction of stiffer penalties for parents whose children, for example, break the law or fail to go school. This was combined with measures to provide advice and support for parents – childcare support for working parents, the setting up of the National Family and Parenting Institute, and the introduction of Sure Start schemes with nurseries and parenting support in the poorest areas to give children a better start in life. The creation of a new Ministry for Children, Young People and Families in 2003 signalled a more focused approach to children and their families. Its blueprint document, *Every Child Matters*,[16] argued for a universal approach to children and family support. The central plank of all these policies is that parents should work in partnership with the state, the voluntary and the commercial sectors, to protect children from harm and to ensure they have opportunities to get on in life, particularly through education.

Equal partners?

This notion of 'partnership' between parents and the state begs the question whether it is a partnership of equals, and whether the contract to receive support in return for exercising responsibilities is a balanced one. The shortfall in terms of support for working parents indicates that this balance has not yet been achieved, but it also raises questions about whether the priorities set by government are the same as those shared by parents. As we show in Chapter 4, parents are less driven by a concern to make work pay than by a concern to do the right thing by their children, especially in relation to the quality of care they can offer them. Traditionally, too, much family support has been targeted on particular problems, such as so-called 'problem parents' or young offenders. This has generated a sense of stigma associated with using family support services and a degree of mistrust based on a fear that the state has the power to take one's children away.[17] In the move to make services accessible the important issues are what sort of support parents want, how they might have a greater say in those services and how trust might be developed. These are questions we consider in Chapter 5.

Moral dilemmas

Law and policy have also carried two further tensions. The first is between acknowledging the diversity of family life whilst also stressing that it is preferable for children to have married parents. So, even though there has been a shift away from seeing divorce as a moral matter, at each point when new legislation has been introduced with the intention of making divorce more straightforward, the political debates that have surrounded its passage have actually justified it as a way of *strengthening* marriage.[18] Such debates routinely assume the position that divorce is a personal tragedy for all involved, especially the children, and that marriage and stability are best for children, a point reinforced by New Labour's first blueprint for family policy, *Supporting Families*, one of whose main proposals was to strengthen marriage whilst recognising that not everyone chose to marry.[19] Empirical research suggests, as we relate later, that there is considerable complexity in how people's commitments operate, but the point here is that these messages place separating and divorcing parents in an intolerable bind. On the one hand, they are expected to consider their children's interests as uppermost; on the other, they are led to believe that they have already practically ruined their children's lives. This intensifies the moral dilemma already facing parents, but without providing the guidance which can help them to think through the 'proper thing to do' in their situation. In other words, parents, having been entrusted with the practical ethics of divorce, find themselves cast as amoral actors. This is why we need a greater understanding of what *does* matter to parents and to their children when they are in these situations.

Equal players?

Just as parenting has acquired much greater political significance, so it has for parents become intensified through children's extended financial dependence but also, it would seem, in terms of emotional significance (see Figure 5, page 21). Where there are conflicts in post-divorce arrangements these are beginning to centre on the rights of fathers to have an equal share to residency (or custody of the child, as it is more commonly known).[20] Increasingly too, as a logical consequence, resolution of the conflict is sometimes to split residency so that a child lives half the time with one parent and half the time with the other. This would, on the face of it, seem to be fair to both parents and encourage a move towards equality of caring responsibilities. However, the reality of most married or cohabiting parenting is neither of equal parenting (nor of equal careers), as we have already shown in Chapter 1. More importantly, the new practice of fairness in post-divorce caring may overlook the perspective of the child on being 'shared' in this way.[21] 'Equality' hides the complexities of family practices and how men, women and children cope with and experience divorce: we need to disaggregate the different experiences of family members, and to know much more of children's experiences of divorce.

The best interests of the child?

The issue of children's interests has become central to the family policy agenda. The Children Act of 1989 secured a duty upon adults to promote the best interests of the child and to be attentive to children's wishes and feelings. In the same year, the United Nations adopted the Convention on the Rights of the Child which set out the basic human rights for children in terms of protection and participation. Its four principles are non-discrimination, the best interests of the child, survival and development, and participation. In these ways, national and international policy moved a long way from the idea that children should be seen but not heard and appears to promote a much more democratic understanding of the child as a citizen. However, the notion of 'the best interests of the child' can serve some very different views of what childhood and children are about. Are children victims in need of protection? Are they potential villains in need of constraint and punishment? Are they our investment as future citizens, workers and parents? Or are they citizens of the present?

Protect or punish?

The 2003 Green Paper *Every Child Matters* proposed a more universal approach to children's protection with universal and multidisciplinary prevention and early intervention, rather than just targeted protection, and it combined these with the goal of ending child poverty and enabling every child to reach their potential. In setting out these aims this important paper also embodied many of the tensions in how we understand children, for example the tension between protection and punishment. To begin with, measures to ensure that children are protected from harm are central. Yet this concern is offset by a youth justice system which is seen by many to be overly punitive.[22] Britain is unusual in Europe in having 10 years as the age of criminal responsibility, and in using custodial sentences for 12–14 year olds even when they have not been persistent offenders. Along with this, the decision to uphold parents' (but not childminders') right to use 'reasonable chastisement' (smacking) on their children has led to accusations of the government contravening its obligations under the UN Convention on the Rights of the Child to build a culture of respect for the human rights of the child.[23]

Listening to children

The second concern with government policies for children is that while the attempts to lift children out of poverty, and to ensure they have access to nurseries and schools and qualifications, have been progressive, are they more about turning children into future worker-citizens than about recognising their rights to be heard as citizens of the present? *Every Child Matters* is a good example of this. It emphasises children's rights to 'enjoying and achieving' but talks much more about achievement than enjoyment. The picture presented in this paper is of education as the basis of employ-ability, and employability as the insurance against poverty and the basis of economic competitiveness. It also stresses the importance of children's voices: the development of a government Children and Young People's Unit has championed the interests of children and their involvement in decision-making structures, responding to a strong lobby, especially from the large children's charities, in favour of respect for children's views.[24] But there are also concerns that these moves can be tokenistic – *Every Child Matters* refers to children's views only in passing, and even less to parents having influence upon the design and delivery of services.

A new normative family?

The power of the post-war male breadwinner family was that it marginalised and often pathologised those who fell outside its frame. Male homosexuality was a crim-inal offence until 1967; along with 'people living in sin' and 'unmarried mothers', same-sex couples were seen as belonging to a different, and lower, moral order. The practices of minority ethnic families were often seen as problematic – mothers from the Caribbean who entered full-time work to support their children were deemed to be neglecting them; South Asian families were not offered services on the assump-tion that they could rely on their extended family networks. The legacy of eugenics meant that it was assumed that disabled people could not make 'fit' parents. How much has all this changed? Is there a new normative family emerging from law and policy where parents are preferably but not necessarily married, where their joint paid work keeps them out of poverty and better enables them to exercise their responsibilities to protect their children and keep them out of trouble? And how far does this new family model embrace formerly excluded groups?

Lone parents

Lone parents, whether never-married or divorced, exemplify the separation of marriage from parenting, and as such, have been central targets in New Labour's efforts to get people off welfare and into work, to lift children out of poverty and to reinforce parental responsibilities. So, although the moral disapproval associated with their lack of marital status has dissipated, they have become, through their need for support and the poverty of their children, a target for state intervention. Some interventions, such as Sure Start, aim to give disadvantaged children a better start. They are part of a broader, work-orientated policy objective to get 70% of lone parents into work by 2010.[25] The problems with this objective reveal in starker form some of the tensions already discussed in the move to the adult worker model. Employment rates for lone parents (mainly mothers) have increased by 8%, from 46% in 1997 to 54% in 2003.[26] This increase represents employment for those who are 'job ready', such as those with higher qualifications, older children or informal childcare support.[27] Many still do not earn a sufficient household income, however, as 71% of lone mothers still rely on some welfare benefit or tax credit.[28] Those in greatest poverty are younger parents with younger children and lower qualifications and who live in localities with low labour market opportunities. Furthermore, many lone mothers, in common with most other mothers, prefer to stay at home rather than go out to work in the first year of their child's life.[29] With lone parents also being disproportionately penalised by anti-social behaviour and truancy orders, many feel pulled in different directions: as good citizens they should be in paid work, but as good mothers they should be at home preventing their children from misbehaving.

If lone parents have been taken out of a 'moralising' frame and replaced in a 'social responsibility' frame, then teenage mothers have similarly had their badge of sexual immorality removed. However, it has been replaced by a different requirement of moral responsibility – to obtain educational qualifications and skills and to be in paid work.

Cohabitees

It is estimated that by 2021 30% of all couples will be cohabiting.[30] According to the British Social Attitudes Survey of 2001, two-thirds of people accepted that cohabitation has become both a prelude and an alternative to marriage. People who cohabit are socially and economically representative of the population as a whole except that they are younger. Contrary to popular belief, cohabitees are generally people who are earning rather than receiving benefits.

Legally, cohabitees do not have the same rights as married people even though many people assume that they do. For example, half of all cohabitees own houses, yet their partners do not have automatic entitlement to a share of that home if the owner dies, or if the pair separate, in the way that a married person would. Nor can they inherit from their partner if no will has been made. Unmarried fathers have a legal responsibility to their children only if they have formally applied for it. Heterosexual cohabitees do not have protection in law, and have not been recognised either in family policy or in the proposals for civil partnership.[31] On the other hand, cohabitees *are* treated as single earner and dependant when it comes to receiving state benefits. The joint assessment of cohabiting sexual partners is one area of welfare where the old principle of the main provider and dependent partner is still maintained.

Minority ethnic parents

There has been much greater acknowledgment of multiculturalism and of the need to counter racism. The Children Act 1989 and the Race Relations Amendment Act 2000[32] place a duty on all public institutions to take measures to prevent racial discrimination. Many government policy documents carry images of a multicultural Britain. *Supporting Families* is no exception – four different family groupings are pictured on the cover, three of which have people from minority ethnic groups. Yet despite its cover, *Supporting Families* does not refer at all to what support for minority ethnic families might mean, or whether their needs and experiences might be different. This omission gives rise to a concern that multiculturalism is seen as having been achieved, rather than as something still to be worked at.[33]

Research reports on minority ethnic families' experiences show how racism, lack of respect for religious or cultural differences and material disadvantages continue to be part of the day to day lives of people of African-Caribbean, Bangladeshi, Indian and Pakistani heritage.[34] This means that issues of protection include concerns about protection from racism. There continue to be inequalities in use of and access to care services in health and social care. For example, black disabled children are more likely to be excluded from school and have less access to services and subsequent employment.[35] The Day Care Trust reports an urgent need for sensitive strategies to track equality and anti-discriminatory practices in the training and recruitment of those who work in services for children.[36] First-, second- and third-generation minority and migrant groups have significant kinship networks and commitments which operate across continents and often go unrecognised in policies for community care or education.[37]

In addition government position-statements and policies in relation to asylum-seekers and, after 9/11, Muslim fundamentalism, often muddy the waters of multiculturalism and race relations. For example, the proposal in 2003 from the Home Office to take the children of illegal migrants into care contradicted the proposals for care and protection of children in *Every Child Matters*. Similarly, requirements for a greater commitment of minority groups to subscribe to 'British norms' and a 'British identity', tend to overplay the fixedness of cultural identities and religious beliefs. Pakistani and Bangladeshi family practices for arranged marriages, for example, are often presented as though they are fixed and pre-modern, where women are victims, rather than part of complex patterns of kin commitment and subject to challenge and revision from women within those communities.[38] It is also the case that these experiences do not feature in much of the research on family lives and personal relationships.

Disabled parents and children

The historic exclusion of disabled adults and disabled children from the right to a family life began to be challenged by the disability movement and others from the

1960s onwards. Disabled parents, in common with other disabled people, are now eligible for direct payments – cash support to buy in services. This has been an important development in giving disabled people greater control and choice over the sorts of assistance that they require, but take-up remains low, particularly amongst minority ethnic groups, and not all direct payments cover parenting needs. Disabled people, too, have been the focus of welfare-to-work policies.

In spite of this, both disabled adults and disabled children continue to be amongst the groups whose needs are most neglected by family policies and this is compounded for minority ethnic families. Shifts in policy which prioritise paid work for adults and educational qualifications for children can serve to displace those for whom standard employment and standard schooling are inappropriate or inaccessible. Parents of disabled children, especially mothers, are more likely to be lone parents and to be unemployed, yet costs of caring for a disabled child can be three times more than for an able-bodied child, and disabled children are even less likely to be consulted about their needs by professionals.[39]

Similarly, disabled parents complain that services are developed *for* them rather than *with* them and assume that they require care rather than assistance. Department of Health policies which have highlighted the children of disabled parents as 'young carers' have had the effect of directing resources through the children's needs. While this recognises their needs as carers, it has had the further effect of displacing their parents and not recognising the webs of care and interdependence between disabled parents and their children.[40]

Same-sex partners
The situation for gay and lesbian partners has improved significantly in law. After years of mobilisation by gay and lesbian organisations Section 28 of the 1988 Local Government Act was repealed in 2003. This had prohibited the promotion of same-sex relationships by local authorities and made it difficult for teachers and social workers to talk positively to young people about homosexuality, or their own sexuality if they were gay or lesbian, for fear of being seen to promote it. In 2004 the age of consent for same-sex relationships was brought into line with that for heterosexuals, at 16. The Adoption and Children Act 2004 enabled gay men and lesbians to adopt. Probably the most far-reaching proposal has been to create a framework for the legal recognition of same-sex couples. This would offer the possibility of civil partnerships to cohabiting gay and lesbian partners to support their commitment and to provide most of the rights and responsibilities afforded to married people, for example in relation to housing and a partner's acquiring legal parental responsibility. This sort of recognition would be important, for example, when visiting partners in hospital or negotiating care help for an elderly partner. Civil partners would also find themselves treated as a single family unit for receipt of income support benefits.

This process of creating civil partnerships is interesting for two reasons. First, it has forced the articulation of what defines a 'partnership' and the nature of its commitment. For example, the consultation paper talks about 'emotional and financial commitments' as the basis of partnership, and in response to a question in the consultation process about whether there was a duty to cohabit for civil partners, the proposals said: 'Cohabitation means living in a shared household. The obligation to cohabit can be achieved by separate homes, which can form one household if this is the customary arrangement for the partners concerned.'[41] This means that a shared residence has become less significant as a marker of commitment than shared finances and emotional commitment. However, the line is drawn at extending civil partnerships to co-resident siblings, home-sharers or adult carers and their cared-for kin, on the basis that such relationships do not have the same case for recognition. All of this raises important questions about how people understand their commitments in the different living circumstances in which they might find themselves – as same-sex couples, as step-parents, as individuals living on their own, as childless couples, and so on. How far does the focus on the sexual couple relationship, as in marriage and in civil partnerships, reflect people's experiences of care and support in their lives? We look at these issues in Chapter 3.

Conclusion

Family policies and laws have begun to reframe the normative model of family and personal relationships. The 'adult worker' model has replaced the 'male breadwinner', and parental, financial and care responsibilities before, during and after marriage have become the new focus of state intervention, with an explicit commitment to serve children's best interests. While marriage continues to be promoted as preferable for parenting, an acknowledgement of the diversity of partnership relationships marks the waning influence of an overarching morality 'from above'. The possibility of civil partnerships for same-sex couples is the most obvious manifestation of this. At the same time, a new moral imperative on the importance of paid work has emerged which connects parental responsibilities, investment in education and children, and the fight against poverty and social exclusion with Britain's economic place in the world. A different sort of partnership has become central to drive this new imperative forward – this time not between individuals, but between the state, parents and the voluntary and commercial sectors. The new frame may be more inclusive, but its priorities of work, education and responsibility place some at greater advantage than others.

The gap between *ought* and *is*
As with all normative models, there are gaps between the *ought* and the *is*. A recurrent example is the different relationships men and women have to the labour market and to the care of children, which has led to parents negotiating a variety of ways of combining work and care. There also seem to be tensions in the balance between the support the state offers and the responsibilities that parents are required to carry out. This points to the central importance of material support, such as income and childcare funding, but it also involves a set of moral considerations. Is the priority of 'making work pay' which inscribes the new morality for parenting,

one which also matters most to parents? Is there true recognition of diversity, or is it only skin-deep? And is the parent–state partnership one of mutual trust? Does the state trust the commitment of parents, do policies reflect the way people's commitment operates, and do parents trust the support which the state and other sectors provide? And where do children's views have a place in this partnership?

At the heart of these questions is a more searching one. In the waning influence of an external moral code, and in the remaking of relations of gender, generation, ethnicity, disability and sexuality, people have had to draw on their own frameworks of what is right and proper to solve their parenting and partnering dilemmas (do I stay at home to look after my child or go out to work, should I get divorced, do I encourage my daughter to have an arranged marriage as I did?). These frameworks may or may not be based in faith or tradition. What, then, should be the aims of government? Should its policies seek to *reflect* the diversity of people's lives and the choices they make, or should it be concerned with *setting* new standards and moral codes? If government does the former, it risks perpetuating the inequalities which exist and influence the decisions people make. For example, if parents are paid to stay at home and look after their children, will this not just reinforce less qualified women's lack of power in the labour market? If it sets a new standard, it risks creating a moral frame which elevates some (those in paid work) and despises others (those not in paid work). And if it does both, as New Labour has done, it will be charged with inconsistency.

What we offer in the next three chapters is not a solution, but a way of rethinking this impasse. Our research has studied the dilemmas of parenting and partnering, how people themselves have articulated these, how they have worked out what to do and what is important to them. Through this we have developed a grounded understanding of the priorities people have and of what matters to them in their relationships of care and commitment. These grounded values provide an alternative approach to thinking about families and personal relationships. This is not simply about reflecting what people do, nor about developing a new moral stand, but about defining some guiding principles out of what it is that matters to people in negotiating and carrying out their commitments of care, and how they themselves deal with the inconsistencies and contradictions of their own lives.

Summary

- The move towards an 'adult worker model' and away from the 'male breadwinner model' in social policy has assumed the centrality of paid work in men and women's lives. However, women's relationship with the labour market is mediated by their care responsibilities.

- Support for work/life balance has been developed, but problems of quality, flexibility and cost remain issues, along with women and men's own preferences and practices in combining work and care.

- The focus of family law has placed men and women as *parents* rather than as spouses. Policies focus more on the regulation of *parenting responsibilities* in relation to children's education and behaviour.

- The 'best interests of the child' has been a consistent theme but interpretations of this differ. There are tensions between protection and punishment, and between children as citizens of the present with voices to be heard and as citizens of the future with exams to be passed.

- To some extent a new normative family is emerging which is heavily rooted in work, economic self-sufficiency, education and good behaviour. It revolves around the adult couple, based on a current or past sexual relationship, and is beginning to recognise same-sex couples. Its embrace is ambivalent in relation to lone parents, families with a disabled member, cohabitees and minority ethnic families.

NOTES

1   See Lewis (2001b) for a more comprehensive study.
2   Williams (1989, 1999); Williams, Popay and Oakley, eds (1999).
3   See Duncan and Williams, eds (2002); Hobson (2004); Mahon (2002) for details of these different countries.
4   Williams, in Knijn and Komter, eds (2004b).
5   See Duncan and Williams, eds (2002); Hobson (2004); Mahon (2002).
6   Quarmby (2003).
7   Crompton, Brockmann and Wiggins, in Park et al., eds (2003); Dench et al. (2002); see also Chapter 6 in Duncan and Edwards (1999).
8   Bryson et al. (2000).
9   TUC (2003).
10 House of Commons Work and Pensions Committee (2003).
11 Dex (2003).
12 Toynbee (2003).
13 Lewis (2001a).
14 ONS (2004d); Barlow et al., in Park et al., eds (2002).
15 Home Office (2003).
16 Department for Education and Skills (2003).
17 Ghate and Hazel (2002).
18 Lewis 2001b.
19 Home Office (1998).
20 Smart (2003a); Smart, Neale and Wade (2001); Phillips (2003).
21 Smart (2003a).

22 For example see Muncie (1999).
23 The Joint Committee on Human Rights (2003) states that 'currently, reasonable chastisement is under review'.
24 Roseneil and Williams (2004); Williams (2004a).
25 Gray (2001).
26 Quarmby (2003).
27 Fimister, ed. (2001).
28 DWP (2003).
29 84% according to Quarmby (2003).
30 Shaw and Haskey (1999) quoted in Barlow et al., in Parks et al., eds (2002).
31 Barlow and James (2004).
32 This was passed after the Macpherson Report (1999) following the death of black teenager Stephen Lawrence at the hands of a group of white youths, and a subsequent campaign by his family to reveal the racism of the police who dealt with the case.
33 Becher and Hussain (2003).
34 Chahal and Julienne (1999); Chahal (2003).
35 Broomfield (2004).
36 Richards and Ince (2000); Daycare Trust (2003).
37 Ackers (2000); Chamberlain, ed. (1998).
38 Hussain and O'Brien (2000).
39 Dobson, Middleton and Beardsworth (2001); Broomfield (2004).
40 Morris (2003); Olsen and Clarke (2003).
41 Women and Equality Unit (2003), p. 37.

3

Connectedness and commitments

This and the next chapter focus on CAVA's research findings. In this chapter we show that although relationships may be changing in shape, these changes have not undermined people's sense of commitment to one another. When faced with dilemmas, people generally negotiate 'the proper thing to do' in and through such commitments, especially with reference to the well-being of their children. The picture of people as individualised and freed of the older constraints of marriage does not account for this connectedness and the influence it has on the choices people exercise in their family lives and personal relationships. We therefore draw out some of the practical ethics which enable people's resilience in the face of change. Far from the dystopian vision of self-seeking individualism and moral decline which fills public debate, we found people who are seeking to create new moral frameworks in which 'fairness' to and 'respect' for others are key aspirations.

The research

Our empirical research on changes in parenting and partnering shows that the picture of self-actualising pioneers or selfish individuals fails to capture the moral texture of family lives and personal relationships in Britain today. Instead, it finds people to be energetic moral actors, embedded in webs of valued personal relationships, working to sustain the commitments that matter to them. We found that the choices people make – when considering how to juggle parenthood with work, or whether to remarry after divorce, for example – are morally informed responses to changes in their circumstances, rather than simple expressions of individual choice or lifestyle. When faced with dilemmas, people draw on repertoires of values about care and commitment in order to work out what, in practice, would be the 'proper thing to do'. This involves complex negotiations and accommodations which are worked out in and through their relationships with others, but also influenced by the opportunities and constraints provided by who and what they are and where they live. There is, in the in-depth interviews we carried out, far *less* evidence of over-weening self-centredness than there are stories of the variety of fine tunings people perform in order to balance a sense of self with the needs of others.

The outcomes of these tunings provide a diverse picture of arrangements for living, caring, working and loving, but this diversity should not be read as moral decline or even as a lack of consensus about what does matter to people. Of course, some people cope better than others, some care much better and some are clearer in their commitments. But in order to understand the moral texture of commitment it is necessary to look beyond marriage and the conjugal couple, for then we can see that it is the shape and texture of contemporary commitments that may be changing – who matters and why – more than their actuality. Commitments extend beyond blood and marriage to households linked through dissolved marriages, cohabitations, through new step-relations and friendships, and across continents following migration and settlement. They register new interpretations of what it is that matters when change happens – for example, how to give children the attentiveness they need, or how to sustain significant relationships. In presenting this more complex picture through our research certain ideas can be seen to recur: connectedness and commitment, negotiation, balance and accommodation, care and support, context and diversity.

We explore these ideas in this chapter and the next through the projects we conducted.[1] All of these focused on an aspect of social change which has significance for family lives and personal relationships, and all looked at 'what matters' to people in the conditions of change in which they found themselves. The projects discussed here are on: kin relationships after separation and divorce; employment and child-care; values of care amongst parents of primary school children; transnational kinship; friendship and non-conventional partnerships; and collective voices in parenting and partnering. They were all qualitative studies, and thus, unlike the statistical and survey material referred to in earlier chapters that provide an extensive picture of social change, this research provides data that helps us understand better the processes and meanings behind change affecting family lives and personal relationships. This chapter focuses on the shape and texture of commitments and connectedness in family lives and friendship while Chapter 4 looks at care and support in the context of the wider issues of employment, localities and culture.

Energetic moral agents

Much of the intensive, in-depth sociological research that has listened to adults and children talk about events in their family lives and personal relationships seems to bear out the idea that, far from exhibiting a decline in values or morality, adults, and children too, are 'energetic moral agents'. That is not to say they moralise, or that they always behave well, but that they spend time weighing up the pros and cons of the consequences of their actions, considering others' perspectives and needs and reflecting on the decisions they make.

Take this extract from a study of divorced couples by Carol Smart and Bren Neale.[2] Here, Stella talks about deciding whether to get back together with her husband, Nick, from whom she had separated. The separation followed her traumatic discovery that he had a long-term relationship with another woman who had had his child. This child was the same age, four, as the younger of her two sons. It was Nick who initiated the idea of getting back together:

> 'When he first said it I got really depressed for two weeks because I thought, "I can't afford not to consider this because of my boys and although I may want to just dismiss this, I'm actually gonna have to think about this." I thought, "I don't want to open all those boxes that I've dealt with and put away. I don't want to have to look at all that again." And I thought, "Well, I'm going to have to," and for a couple of weeks I got very depressed and I did open all the boxes again and look at everything and then I just thought, "That's the best decision I ever made in my life and I'm really glad I did." I'm not saying it was all bad, of course it wasn't, we had some great times, but … I didn't realise how submissive he'd made me.'[3]

The careful weighing-up of how much the boys might want their father back (they had a good relationship with him which she facilitated), of how much she felt she had been through, of the hard work it had been to create a new identity for herself – all of this is common in the accounts researchers hear about how people manage these defining moments of their lives. Whether they are talking about divorce, or whether to take on the care of a frail older parent, how to have the baby cared for when they go back to work – it seems that what many people share is not an agreement on a set of abstract moral imperatives, but a weighing-up of the given situation. People negotiate within certain moral and social guidelines according to the context they are in. The question they ask themselves is not so much 'What *ought* I to do', but 'How should I deal with this? What, in the circumstances, is the proper thing to do?'[4] Far from being demoralised, there is a palpable moral texture to their lives. And while, like Stella, people are concerned about their own self-fulfilment, this is embedded within the needs of others. Smart and Neale drew from their research the following guidelines which appeared to frame their interviewees' considerations about whether or not to divorce:[5]

- The present quality of the relationship with their partner and the nature of it in the past;
- The effect on other close relationships (especially children but also grandparents);
- Whether it is the right time (for example, in terms of ages of children);
- The extent of harm/benefit to all those involved.

This is not to say that *everyone* is equally oriented to the needs of others, but what is being challenged is the idea that 'the ethic of individual self-fulfilment and achievement is the most powerful current in modern society'.[6] If people are embedded in their relationships with others, and yet also subject to change, what does this mean for their commitments?

Reconfiguring the shape and texture of commitments

'We went out for a family meal about six months ago with my brother and his wife. And there is my ex-husband sat on one side of me, my current husband on the other, my ex-husband's girlfriend opposite me, and the children sort of bouncing – with merely a batting of an eyelid, they moved as easily between Jemma and me and Mark and Colin – that's actually down to me.'[7]

The effect of the 1989 Children Act was to emphasise shared parenting after divorce, and although this now happens in all sorts of different ways, it has presented people with new dilemmas about how to negotiate those relationships associated with their marriage or partnership. How, for instance, do parents maintain their children's relationship with their ex-parents-in-law? Smart and Neale's research on post-divorce relationships provides an informative lens through which to look at how far divorce breaks up families and severs commitments.[8]

Kin-keeping

They found that many divorced parents, usually but not exclusively women, would take it upon themselves to perform an active 'kin-keeping' role after divorce in order to sustain relationships, not just with the other parent, but with grandparents and in-laws as well. However, this was not inevitable: sometimes children were independent enough to sustain such relationships without help; sometimes divorce provided a parent or grandparent with the opportunity to withdraw from what had been a problematic relationship. Sustaining post-divorce relationships where children were involved demonstrated a considerable degree of accommodation to the needs of others. Grandparents often provided much needed financial and practical childcare support to parents when they might most need it, and where they were able to maintain a policy of neutrality about their child's separation or divorce this could facilitate the survival of strained relationships and even strengthened them. What also kept relationships with ex-kin going was their existing quality, where good relationships based upon affection, kindness and mutual support had been built up over time.

Relationships with ex-partners

Maintaining a relationship with an ex-partner in order to share post-divorce parenting is not always straightforward. Certain conditions make it especially difficult: where there has been violence, or where trust has completely broken down, or where divorce runs counter to a family's faith. Where it does work, it is because ex-partners are able to re-orient themselves towards each other, as Leon describes:

'Even though you separate or divorce, you still have a relationship. Whatever your relationship is depends on the two individuals – even if you have children involved, there is a

relationship involved, even if you have a distant relationship. I think once I decided very early on, and Jill the same, that the children – we were looking after the children – and you can't do that without considering the needs of the other person, and it's water under the bridge why you got divorced, and the financial side, because you have to consider each other's needs really, very much so.[9]

Divorce does not therefore inevitably spell rupture. Post-divorce kin relationships show the *changing shape* of commitments as they extend across households no longer linked by marriage. The practical ethics which are important in these situations are based on attentiveness to others' needs, adaptability to new identities, and a spirit of reparation. At the same time, these ethics, and the dilemmas for parents with children about re-partnering after divorce provide evidence of the *changing texture* of commitments. While almost half of divorced men and just over a third of divorced women go on to remarry and create new families, others do not, but nevertheless work out different ways of 'doing' post-divorce life.[10] In their study, Smart and Neale found that parents opted for a number of alternatives to remarriage: the 'detached' where relationships with new partners were either discounted or conducted away from the children; the 'linked' where the two new partners maintain their own separate households; and the 'cohabiting'. Often an important reason given for pursuing any of these options was 'for the sake of the children'.

Detached
Heather was 'detached' because she felt it was the best way to maintain stability for her children:

'I have had partnerships but none that have got to the stage where it's been [serious]. I keep it very separate to my children … I'm very old-fashioned like that … I know girls who have lots of "uncles" and they get involved with the kids … but I think you have to be very serious before you do that.'[11]

Linked
'Linked' relationships were close partnerships where each person retained their own separate residence. These forms of relationship are increasingly common amongst all sorts of different groups and are sometimes referred to as 'LATs' (living-apart-together).[12] It means that some of the activities which are conventionally thought to represent 'commitment' such as shared domesticity and domestic space and finances, are carried out separately, but, in these parents' cases, this did not mean they were any the less committed to the relationship. Often it was a way of maintaining (or in some cases repairing) the integrity of their own parenting relationship with their children, as Chris describes:

'What makes it work? Probably the fact that we haven't moved in together. Lucy was aware that I wouldn't have been prepared to have her kids. I quite like the kids but … the family are fairly argumentative … I would have felt uncomfortable living with it and that

was basically the fundamental reason … She's just got one at home and, you know, if [my son] moves out, then I'm fairly sure that we'll probably move in [together] one way or another.'[13]

Lucy and Chris also had other important family commitments and living apart enabled them to balance their children's needs and their own identities as parents with their responsibilities to others. In this instance, it is possible to see how the mutual appreciation of others' needs – not only those of the other partner but their responsibilities too – are a crucial contribution to a sense of commitment. The fact that Lucy and Chris chose not to aggregate some of the practical strands of that commitment (domesticity, finances, parenting the other person's children) did not diminish the commitment itself; rather, it changed its shape and its texture, so that its various strands interwove to construct a different mesh to contain the new partnership.

Cohabitation

Cohabitation and remarriage are the other ways in which post-divorce parents choose to re-partner. Smart and Neale found that of all the different partnership patterns, cohabitation was probably less 'worked through'. This should not be taken to reflect upon all forms of cohabitation, which can be seen as a *prelude* to marriage for younger couples, which may or may not last, as a *sequel* to marriage following separation, or as a *substitute* for marriage, and where, as Jane Lewis's study shows, commitments are as deeply felt and achieved as in married relationships.[14] However, Smart and Neale's separated parent interviewees found that sometimes cohabitation involved a partner moving into someone else's household; sometimes people felt they were offering their children the benefit of an additional adult presence (perhaps a male role model); some preferred the lack of taken-for-grantedness which cohabitation offered in contrast to their experience of marriage; whereas for others its very lack of taken-for-grantedness created insecurities.

Remarriage

Remarriage for divorced parents was therefore not their only option and may have demanded more of a rationale than their first marriage as young adults. Remarriage typically involved not simply a public statement of mutual love and commitment, but also financial and social status and security (especially for women), an opportunity to make a symbolic break with the old marriage and spouse (and perhaps the partner's ex-marriage and ex-spouse), and to make a fresh start.

It is difficult to understand these negotiations to re-partner by separated or divorced parents as free choices or as unencumbered lifestyle preferences. Certainly they were freer of normative expectations that they should reproduce, for their own or for their new partner's children, the conditions of the conventional stable married household. However, they worked with a 'complex calculus of commitments rather than thinking of commitment as having to mean accepting a pre-designed package'.[15] Since many put their children's needs first, these were difficult rather than free choices. They were also hard won in so far as they were being worked out under new freedoms and constraints – where biological parents are expected to share parenting after divorce, where marriage and cohabitation are not the only frames for sexual relationships, where public debates associate lone parenting, divorce and step-parenting with children's educational and emotional disadvantage. It may seem that in discussing the ways in which people coped with changes in their lives we are over-looking the pull of more difficult and complex emotions such as jealousy, resentment, rivalry, revenge and the practices of manipulation and oppression which mark people's exprinces of family lives and personal relationships. These were certainly present in people's lives, but we were concerned to find what values and ethics *enabled* people's emotional resilience.

None of this speaks to the experiences and views of children. We do that below, but first we draw out some of the new meanings and metaphors that have become important in these new patterns of commitment and connectedness: the significance of friendship; the practices of fairness; and children's views and experiences.

Sex, love and friendship

A number of the features of post-divorce parents' lives reappear in the lives of others who are neither divorced, nor parents, nor necessarily heterosexual. Cohabitation, for example, is common amongst young adults with or without children.[16] However, an arrangement which appears to be gaining ground amongst younger and older people is living one's life without a co-resident partner, as in the case of the 'detached' couples above. Irene Levin's study of 'living-apart-together' couples in Norway and Sweden suggests that this phenomenon is the consequence of the dis-aggregating of the four sequential elements of entry into normative heterosexual family life: marriage, living together, sex and parenthood.[17] Sex and marriage became uncoupled in the 1960s, marriage and parenthood by the 1980s, and now sex and living together are no longer essential bedfellows. Different conditions may occasion this arrangement: where couples have existing family commitments, or where they work in different places, where they worry about repeating a mistake of past relationships, where they are retired and want to maintain the integrity of their own houses, cherished belongings and relationships with children and grand-children, or simply, where proximity breeds irritation. What this shows is that the growth of 'singletons', which has represented one of the biggest increases in house-hold types over the past 30 years, involving almost one-third of households in 2001 (see Figures 1, 2, 3 and 4 in Chapter 1, pages 12–13), should not necessarily be equated with people's being less connected to each other. Many may be embedded in significant non-residential relationships. It should be added that although this is seen as a new phenomenon, the practice of having a 'visiting' partner or co-parent has been one of the enduring patterns (but not the only pattern) of partnering and parenting amongst people of African-Caribbean origin in Britain. Nonetheless, the same point obtains: that these relationships too entail commitment.[18]

An ethic of friendship

Sasha Roseneil and Shelley Budgeon's CAVA study focused on this growing group of people who live and love without a co-resident partner. Their project about people living in non-conventional partnerships found that the rationale of many of the people they interviewed who favoured living and loving without a co-resident part-ner was also associated with making *friends* much more central to their networks of care and support. When they did, then friends were valued over lovers, kin or sexual relationships for their emotional and practical significance, as one 28-year-old woman said, 'I think a friendship is for life, but I don't think a partner is – I'd marry my friends. They'd last longer.'[19] In a sense, where the normative post-war nuclear family expected everything to happen under one marital roof – sexual relationship, emotional support, companionship, and parenting – here we can see these processes happening under different roofs and with different people at different stages of their life course. What was also significant in practices of friendship was the blurring of friendship and lover relationships. Lovers became friends and friends became lovers. Another interviewee in this study, Polly, a single parent in her mid-30s with a daugh-ter, had set up home with a friend, Karen, also in her mid-30s, who was also single and had two daughters of similar age. Both are heterosexual, and, as Karen explains, are committed to jointly providing a stable home for their children whilst also help-ing out with each other's childcare, especially around work:

> '*I was in a long relationship for 13 years. We've been separated for three years now so I've been on and off single. I've had a variety of boyfriends and it's been fantastic ... I don't want to tie myself up totally to anybody, but last year I did have somebody who came into my life who was very special, but that was so terrifying ... I said, you know, it can wait, it doesn't have to happen now. This is more important here – my security for my girls ... I don't need to go diving back into anything like that, for a long time. So it's not a major part of me ... No. I'm really enjoying this moment and I enjoy finding somebody new that comes along for a short term but I don't involve them and try not to involve them too much with what's here.*'[20]

Roseneil and Budgeon suggest that their interviewees can be seen as examples of individualisation in that they were freed of the expectations of conventional sexual or kin relations. However, they see this development as part of a slightly different shift happening in 'heteronormative intimacy'. This is where those practices based on co-resident, lifelong, romantic heterosexual love relationships are being displaced by different practices, such as not living with one's lover, and making friends rather than a sexual relationship the basis of the give and take of day-to-day care. Roseneil analyses this development as part of a 'queering' of heterosexual relationships.[21] That is to say, values and practices of intimacy and care which developed in gay and lesbian communities have influenced those of straight people. So, for example, an 'ethic of friendship', where networks of friends/lovers/ex-lovers form the basis for care and support, emerged out of gay and lesbian communities, partly as a conse-quence of not being able to rely on the support of families of origin, but partly out of a belief in the possibility of choosing one's friends and family. Such networks are often termed 'families of choice'.[22] They provided a source of strength to, and were strengthened by, the HIV/AIDS crisis from the 1980s, and later, support for gay and lesbian parenting. As such, these practices of support added to the repertoire of norms and values that have been available to both gay people and heterosexuals. Other small-scale living experiments, not confined to any particular sexual group, have added to this repertoire in similar ways – the communes of the 1960s and 70s and subsequent alternative communities, the present-day practice of sharing accommodation and domesticity, common amongst young adults who are marrying later and do not have the resources to live on their own.[23] Roseneil and Budgeon found, for example, that a belief in an ethic of friendship was articulated by their interviewees who lived without a sexual partner whether they were male or female, gay or straight.

Blurring family and friends

This evidence of the importance of friendship would seem to support one of the tenets of the individualisation thesis: that changes in intimacy have seen a move away from the significance of *fixed, given* or *ascribed* relationships towards ones which are more *fluid, chosen* or *floating*. However, Ray Pahl's empirical study of friendship questions this distinction between given and chosen relationships.[24] He argues that the distinction which sees a move away from given relationships, as represented by kin, to chosen relationships, as represented by friends, is wrong on two counts. First, there is more 'suffusion', or blurring, between friends and family in people's lives than has been recognised in research on kinship or social networks. And second, the idea that 'given' represents the traditional and that 'chosen' represents the new is also mistaken, as patterns of fusion between friends and family members also existed in the past. For example, people in the eighteenth and nineteenth centuries seemed to regard their servants or co-residential farm workers as part of their family. Furthermore, Pahl argues that it is only by looking at the extent of *commitment* in relationships that we can begin to grasp both *who* is important and *how* they are important in what he calls people's 'personal communities'. In his study he found that some people had many different types of friends in their personal communities, whilst others had just a few companions or fun-friends, or one or two very close friends, or a small number of soul-mates with larger groups of companions. In addition, their friends and family emerged in different permutations of closeness, where, for some people, both individual friends and individual family members featured as equally significant.

For many people, then, friends play an important, even central, role in their commitments and sense of belonging. The blurring of friends and family, according to Pahl, and of friends and lovers, according to Roseneil and Budgeon, is what marks many people's personal communities and their connection to the social world. This may seem an obvious point when we think about who our loved ones are, but the empirical details above show the limitations of arguments which see social change mainly taking place through the transformation of intimacy in the adult couple sexual relationship.[25] This neglects the significance of other, lateral, relationships, as well as generational attachments and commitments between parents and children, which, as the post-divorce study showed, play as important a role in defining people's sense of themselves and belonging. These studies of friendship reinforce the point that diversity in the shape of people's commitments does not lead to a weakening of commitment or connectedness. In addition, as Pahl notes, they throw a different light on the nature of social cohesion. It is often assumed by politicians and theorists that the maintenance of *kin* ties is the building block of social cohesion, as strong kin ties are assumed to equal strong communities, and strong communities to equal a strong and stable society. Any weakening or changing of kin ties therefore portends social disintegration. This assumption fails to recognise the very thing that these studies show: that connectedness operates in more various ways than simply through conjugality, sexual intimacy and blood.[26]

Friendships as metaphor

In spite of these sociological refinements of our understanding of friendship, it is interesting that the metaphor of friendship is commonly used to talk about the quality of relationships between kin, in-laws, siblings, and parents and their children.[27] To describe one's brother, or partner's mother, or son's girlfriend as 'more like a friend, really' is regarded as an accolade, and it says much about the qualities we might seek in a good relationship: confiding, sharing, communicative, fun, non-judgemental, mutual, even equal. Of course, it can work the other way too: a good friend might be described as 'more like a sister'. Smart and Neale in their research on post-divorce relationships between kin suggest that a new ethic is emerging in the capacity to sustain relationships, in which:

> '*The core element would appear to be the extent to which central relationships transcend the formal status of a legal tie (e.g. mother-in-law to son-in-law) and move onto terrain more associated with friendship...liking, respect, mutuality and shared interests.*'[28]

Research from Lancaster University by Langford and colleagues on teenage children and their parents shows that parents and young people have strong ideals about democratic, equal relationships, based on negotiated and open communication, and how 'friendship' is consistently invoked as the basis of the ideal family relationship.[29] A 14-year-old boy says approvingly of his relationship with his parents: 'They become more of good friends as you get older.'[30] Parents, too, used this vocabulary of companionship to describe what they valued in their relationships with their children. Does the vocabulary of friendship mean that there has been a qualitative shift in the texture of family lives away from the assumed authority of husband over wife and adult over child and towards greater egalitarianism and democracy?

The Lancaster study above showed that parents invested significantly in their children's lives, and that children valued being able to talk and communicate with their parents. However, it was with their mothers that they mainly achieved this. Fathers found themselves in a more ambiguous role, caught between experiencing the loss of intimacy with children growing up, and being placed in, and often accepting, the role of family disciplinarian. At the same time they were attempting to break with the model of paternal discipline they had experienced as teenagers. The research also found that communication and disclosure between parents and children tended to be one-sided and to focus on the young person's life. For young people, the value of open communication was a recognition and respect for their views, their own life, for their being a person in their own right. While parents also valued the idea of greater companionship, in practice the temptation was to use it as a way of monitoring their children's attitudes and maintaining control, and it was this that young people recognised and resisted. The aspirations towards democracy are significant, but what this study demonstrates is the way different tensions in the relationships and practices between mothers and fathers, and between children and their mothers and fathers, are intertwined. Unravelling the voice of children out of this has been an important recent development in research, and one that offers an insight into what values these aspirations towards democratic relationships might hold.[31]

Fairness, care and respect

What is it that matters to young people in their relationships with adults? Again, divorce and the reconstitution of families after divorce provide examples in which family members find themselves having to think through and reflect upon the nature of their relationships. From their studies of children's experiences after divorce, Bren Neale, Carol Smart and Amanda Wade suggest that four interlinked ethics emerged from the views and experiences children had: [32]

- Fairness
- Care
- Respect
- Trust

Underlying their research is a view of children as competent moral actors able to express their own views in matters that affect them. They found that children had a very refined sense of what was fair and not fair in, for example, arrangements for seeing parents, or how they were treated. In terms of the arrangements for how they should spend time with parents, they assessed the situation with regard to the practical circumstances of who had more time for them, who lived nearer their friends, and so on, as well as the needs of all affected:

> *'Dad doesn't feel it's fair me spending more time at Mum's, but it does work out fairly because he's got all his meetings to go to and I'd be really fed up and wanting to go home or see my friends. It means I don't have to spend too much time with my dad, but I've still got him, I still see him.'* Beth (14) [33]

Fairness operates in tandem with care and respect in what these young teenagers, who have experienced divorce, have to say about what family means to them:

> *'People that are close to you and love you and care about you, care how you feel and just want you to be happy ... We've got a relationship where we can tell Mum everything. My parents don't tell me what to do; they let me live my own life.'* Quentin (13)

> *'A mum needs to be loving and kind, she needs to be there, take care of you. You need to be able to talk to her. For dads, it's the same sort of thing really.'* Sally (12)[34]

Children in Neale and Smart's study preferred openness, communication and shared understanding to being told what was what and what to do. They wanted to be listened to, trusted, taken seriously, kept informed and brought into decision-making. Being cared for is important but it is not enough on its own. It needs to be accompanied by an ethic of respect – where children are accepted as having their own identities, feelings and preferences.

This can create dilemmas – how open should parents be? How much do children need to know? Children wanted to be able to trust their parents to manage things, but did not want to be overburdened with their parents' emotions or conflicts, or treated as go-betweens. Similarly, they did not want to have to make decisions on their own (although, in fact, where children had not been listened to, they did want to be able to exert their own choice). Participation and recognition of their voice were important, rather than control.[35]

Fairness in step-families and cohabitation

In their qualitative study, Jane Ribbens-McCarthy, Ros Edwards and Val Gillies also found a recurring theme of fairness in the practices of parents who live with or marry new partners after divorce or separation.[36] What fairness involved for parents was something they had actively to work towards. For example, ensuring that your step-children saw their mother regularly meant having to be flexible to others' needs, but it was done in the interests of being fair to both parties. Secondly, fairness was some-thing that needed to be seen to be done. When a new partner moved in to an exist-ing household with a parent and children, it was not deemed fair for the new partner to be involved in disciplining the children until he or she had got close to and been accepted by the children. Thirdly, fairness operated within a boundary of an *inclusive* unit, drawing in ex-partners and their children whether related through biology or marriage, or neither. Fourthly, within this unit fairness meant treating children not only equally but also according to their needs and this might be determined by their age, position in the family, or current concerns. And, fifthly, in weighing up fairness for adults and fairness for children, children's needs came first. Nonetheless, putting these versions of fairness into practice also involved significant gender differences, with men seeing themselves as provider and role model for the children and women taking overall responsibility for the children's emotional and practical well-being.

Similarly, Lewis's study of two generations of married and cohabiting couples

found that for the younger age group issues of fairness were paramount in the allocation of time and money to themselves too, although in practice the allocation was
not even between partners.[37] Women did more unpaid work in the home than men,
and men had more leisure time. Men tried to compensate by doing particularly
unpopular jobs or being supportive. Although this did not level the imbalance, it
meant that the issue was on the table for discussion, and in this symbolic sense, these
young couples were less caught in fixed gender roles. However, democracy remained
a possibility rather than a reality.

Fair shares?

Simon Duncan and Lise Saugeres's research, which we report fully in the next chapter, looked at mothers' decisions about combining paid work with motherhood.[38]
Their findings qualify the extent to which men and women are now freed from fixed
ideas about gender and marriage. In asking people for the reasoning behind the ways
they shared household and care work, they found that fixed ideas about women's
biological or psychological attributes for caring play a significant part in their
decision-making. This was especially the case among those women who favoured
staying at home over paid work, but it also influenced those who went out to work
or those who were more career-minded. Although working and career mothers
placed an emphasis on negotiating a fair distribution of tasks with their partner, this
was subject to heavily gendered ideas about female/male preferences and suitabili-
ties. Interchangeability between men's and women's care roles seemed to be possible
only where there was a political commitment by both partners to gender equality.

A number of these issues of 'fairness', 'children's best interests' and gender
differences also emerge in a recent development in parenting after divorce – that of
shared residence for children.

Fairness and children's interests: the case of shared residence

Chapter 2 noted how the 1989 Children Act established the principles that in family
law the welfare of the child is paramount and that parenthood continues after
divorce. These principles dovetailed with a cultural shift in which mothers and
fathers appear to prioritise their emotional investment in their children, during and
after marriage (see Figure 5 on page 21). They have also been heightened by government policies which emphasise the importance of parental responsibilities – in
helping children achieve at school, in ensuring they are well-behaved, and so on. At
the same time, there are still significant gender differences in the care which mothers and fathers provide for their children.[39] These are differences which emerge from,
amongst other things, both gendered assumptions and the constraints of paid working practices and limitations in childcare provision. Divorce highlights the tensions
between the emotional investments parents place in their children and the acutality
of providing practical daily care. Where once it was assumed that care would fall to

the mother, this no longer holds. One form of resolution, which has become the focus of recent debate, is for children to share their residence in both parents' houses by spending part of a week with one and part with another, or possibly a week with one and a week with the other. Whilst this may resolve some issues of fairness between mothers and fathers, what does it mean for children?

In their research on the views of children who were living in a shared residence arrangement, Wade and Smart looked at 'fairness'.[40] They found that when children discussed the positives and negatives of the arrangements they were in, their notion of fairness turned on how *they* could be fair to both their parents:

> *'I think pretty much when they split up they decided that I should spend equal time at both houses or else it wouldn't really be fair. [This way] nobody's got an advantage with me.'*
> James (9)

> *'It's fair to everybody I think. Because I see the same amount of my mum and my dad.'*
> Josh (9)

> *'I'm equally attached to both parents, so if I didn't see one of them as much as I saw the other, I suppose I'd feel guilty, really, for spending more time with one parent than the other.'* Andrijka (10)

Children would work hard to ensure that neither parent lost out. However, in discussing the practicalities of such arrangements some children articulated problems. Older children wanted more time for themselves and their friends rather than sharing it between parents; others found it exhausting being on the move and having to remember to take everything with them that they would need for the next few days. Others did not feel settled in one parent's place because it did not contain their belongings. In other words, the concept of fairness with which they worked was one which did not necessarily include themselves. Their interests could be met only if *their* needs were made part of the resolution of fairness. In cases where shared residence worked, it was where the needs of children were put first, where there was flexibility over arrangements and these could be reviewed, and where children felt equally at home in both households.

At a more general level, these cases show that the issue of how children's voices might be listened to, their experiences and feelings respected, and their needs given priority, is the key to enabling children to manage divorce as one of a range of challenging events they may encounter in their lives.[41]

Summary

- In contrast to arguments which assert that changes in family life have led to a loss of commitment and an increase in selfish individualism, our research found that people seek to sustain the relationships they value. When faced with dilemmas they generally negotiate 'the proper thing to do' in and through their commitments to others, especially with reference to the well-being of their children. The picture of people as individualised and freed of the constraints of marriage does not account for this connectedness and its influence on the variety of fine tunings people perform in order to balance their sense of self with the needs of others.

- The shape of people's commitments may be different today in so far as they are less dependent on blood or marriage ties and may extend across different households linked by dissolved marriages, reconstituted families, non-resident partners and transnational kin. There may be more blurring of kin, ex-kin, sexual partners and friendships in people's relationships. There is also a blurring of those significant relationships which are given and those which are chosen. Little of this indicates a loss of commitment itself, but rather suggests that the mesh of those commitments which contain people's close, caring and intimate relationships is patterned differently. This means we have to rethink the assumption that it is simply stable families based on married couples who form the building blocks for strong communities and social cohesion. Care and commitment cross the boundaries of blood, marriage, residence, culture and country.

- The practical ethics of attentiveness to others' situations, accommodating one's own needs to those of others, adaptability to others' changing identities, and being non-judgemental enable people to find ways of coping with their family lives and personal relationships, even though they may have found those transitions hard. Children value fairness, respect, care, communication and trust in coping with changes in their family lives. These values indicate the moral texture of people's commitments and what matters to them in providing and receiving care and support. They constitute a compassionate realism in people's given circumstances. They are the practical ethics which facilitate resilience to change.

- For some, the ethic of friendship is very significant; this places a premium on friends as the source of everyday care and support. For many, 'friendship' acts as an important metaphor which invokes the quality of relationships marked by closeness, confiding, sharing and equality. At the same time, as people aspire to greater democracy in their relationships, care responsibilities are unevenly balanced between men and women, and children's views and voices are yet to be heard clearly.

NOTES

1   See Appendix 2 for a description of the CAVA research programme and its methodology. See www.leeds.ac.uk/cava for the Working Paper Series. We also include here references to other qualitative research.

2   Smart and Neale (1999). The following section draws largely on the corpus of work by Smart, Neale and Wade on divorce from both CAVA and the Centre for Research on Family, Kinship and Childhood at the University of Leeds (www.leeds.ac.uk/family). See especially: Neale and Smart (1998, 2001, 2004); Neale, Wade and Smart (1998); Smart (2000, 2003a, 2003b, 2003c, 2004a, 2004b); Smart and Neale (1997); Smart, Neale and Wade (1999, 2001).

3   Smart and Neale (1999), p. 122.

4   The 'proper thing to do' was the formulation used by Janet Finch and Jennifer Mason in Finch (1989) and Finch and Mason (1993) in their studies of kinship obligations. See also Sevenhuijsen (1999).

5   Smart and Neale (1999), p. 119.

6   Beck and Beck-Gernsheim (2002), p. 22.

7   Neale and Smart (2004).

8   Neale and Smart (2004).

9   Smart (2003a), p. 8.

10 ONS (2004e); ONS (2004d).

11 Neale and Smart (2004).

12 Levin (2004) discusses this further.

13 Neale and Smart (2004).

14 See Lewis (2001b).

15 Neale and Smart (2004).

16 Barlow, *et al.*, in Parks *et al.*, eds (2002).

17 Levin (2004).

18 See Reynolds, in Carling *et al.*, eds (2002).

19 Roseneil (2003).

20 Roseneil and Budgeon (2004), p. 151.

21 Roseneil (2000a, 2000b).

22 Weeks, Heaphy and Donovan (2001); Nardi and Schneider (1998); Dunne, in Silva and Smart, eds (1999); Weston (1991). Important here too are children who are brought up by friends and non-parent relatives, estimated to be around 300,000 at any one time – Richards and Tapsfield (2003).

23 Heath (2004).

24 Pahl and Spencer (2004).

25 This is a theme of Giddens (1992).

26 Neale and Smart (2003). Roseneil and Budgeon (2004) call this 'networks and flows of love, care and intimacy'.

27 See discussion in Roseneil (2000b).

28 Neale and Smart (2004).

29 Langford *et al.* (2001); Gillies, Ribbens-McCarthy and Holland (2001); Warin *et al.* (1999).

30 Langford *et al.* (2001), p. 32.

31 Alanen and Mayall (2001); James and Prout, eds (1997).

32 Neale and Smart (2001); Smart, Neale and Wade (2001).

33 Neale and Smart (2001), p. 14.

34 Neale and Smart (2001), p. 14.

35 This theme of fairness and respect also emerges in a study of boys aged 11–16 by Frosh, Phoenix and Pattman (2002).

36 Ribbens-McCarthy, Edwards and Gillies (2003).

37 Lewis (2001b).

38 See Duncan (2003).

39 Duncan (2003).

40 Wade and Smart, in Jensen and McKee, eds (2003).

41 Flowerdew and Neale (2003).

4

Care, diversity and contexts

The commitment and connectedness discussed in Chapter 3 were seen largely in the context of changes within and across households. This chapter focuses on areas subject to the external worlds of work and community and finds that here, moral questions in decision-making which are rooted in people's gendered and cultural identities and their commitments to others assume great significance. To begin with, we draw on research on how women combine mothering with paid work. That leads into a discussion about the significance of local context in the decisions people make about parenting and partnering, and then to questions of diversity, culture and change. We end with research that looks at how parents find support beyond family and friends. As in Chapter 3, the aim is to draw out and understand the values that matter to people in the context of changes in parenting and partnering.

Balancing acts: care and work

Simon Duncan's CAVA research[1] explores what he calls 'gendered moral rationalities', that is, how mothers understand the 'proper thing to do' in relation to taking up paid work and caring for their children. His work looks at the processes and meanings which attach to and shape the decisions women make when faced with this issue. While there are differences in whether mothers work full time, part time or not at all, and in what kind of childcare support they prefer, some things are held in common. With or without partners, mothers' decisions are based, first and foremost, on doing *the right thing for their children*. Central to this is their mother/worker identity. So, if your understanding of being a good mother means being a provider for your child, you are more likely to find full-time work an acceptable option. But if being a good mother means 'being there' for your child, then you are more likely to want to work part time or, if you have pre-school children, not at all. This understanding of what it means to be a good mother is also influenced by your social networks, ethnicity and culture, as well as by the local conditions and customs of male and female employment and caring. Class also has an influence, although some strategies are shared by women of different class backgrounds.

Mother/worker identities

The cases below illustrate the range of mother/worker identities that women express: being primarily a mother, being primarily a worker, or integrating, or adapting to, a combined mother/worker identity.

Sylvia is a 24-year-old white, working-class lone mother living in a public housing estate in Moulescoomb, on the periphery of Brighton. She has two children under three who see their father at weekends. She would like to work but feels that this would conflict with what she feels are her children's needs and her maternal responsibility to be there for them:

> '*I'd love to go out to work, I'd love to go back full time … I think I'd be better off financially if I was working than I am now because I only get £68 a week on benefit. My sister gets £185 a week working in a nursing home and I think I could live off that.*'[2]

In arriving at her decision, she was influenced by her mother and her close family network, whom she sees on a daily basis:

> '*My mum is a one parent and she thinks, like most old people, that if you have children you should be with them. You don't have children to bugger off and leave them with someone else is how she sees it. She didn't do it. Sometimes I agree with her. That's the idea, isn't it, of parenting, being with them, isn't it? Well I think it is. Like, you know, I would go to work and not see the kids all day and just see them in the evenings.*'[3]

Although she has an economic incentive to work, it is countered by stronger moral values of her own and the views of her social networks about what is right for children. However, Sylvia's reasoning, which was common to other white unqualified working-class women, partnered and unpartnered, is similar to that of a group of middle-class white women living in a relatively prosperous inner suburb of Leeds. Betty, a highly qualified white graduate, says:

> '*It was like there were two choices, either I get a job and pursue my career or I get married and decide to have a family and put my energies into that.*'[4]

Like Sylvia, she couldn't see the point of having babies if you weren't going to look after them yourself. This is in contrast to Maxine, who lives in Burnley, a town in an area with a strong tradition of working mothers in the cotton industry, although the industry no longer exists. She is white, 33, and as a full-time staff nurse she earns more than her resident partner, a lorry driver working unsocial hours. She has two children of eight and twelve who are looked after out of school by a combination of a childminder and her partner. Her sense of self as a worker is very important to her mothering because this gives her 'more of a purpose … I'm not just a mum or just a wife, I'm a nurse as well and I'm me.'

Gill, 41, is a white middle-class university lecturer with a nine-year-old child, living in Hebden Bridge; like Burnley, a former mill town, but one which has been thoroughly gentrified since the 1970s and where parents have access to professional jobs in Leeds and Manchester. Her partner is self-employed and he and a childminder look after the child while Gill works. However, in common with many of the mothers interviewed she felt a real tension around her mother/worker identity:

> *'People in the area rarely see me as Michael's mother which makes me feel terribly guilty – but I can't leave work early to get to the school gates by half past three. I relish it when I can.'*

Cathy is 30, of African-Caribbean origin, and lives in Chapeltown, an inner-city area of Leeds. She is a nursery officer working long part-time hours, with four children under 16 who are looked after by her resident partner, relatives or nursery care when she works. She says she feels a 'great sense of self-worth when I'm working … it's like, I'm trying to be a really good role model for my children'. In common with other (although not all) African-Caribbean mothers she sees paid work as being complementary to good mothering, and also as part of her cultural heritage.[5] Alex, another African-Caribbean mother, explains her reason for going back into full-time work after maternity leave:

> *'Black mothers have always worked and it was expected that I would be no different because there's this cultural expectation for black mothers that I work.'*

What kind of childcare?

When it came to decisions about childcare provision, the research revealed a similar pattern. Even though mothers had different preferences, their processes of moral reasoning placed a high value on the affective qualities that different childcare options could offer. Women whose identities were more strongly rooted in motherhood than in paid work were, unsurprisingly, likely to feel that they as mothers were best placed to provide this care. However, the converse did not follow, for a preference for informal care, by partners, relatives or childminders, was articulated by working-class mothers with a strong paid-work orientation. The lower costs and greater convenience often strengthened preferences for informal care, but did not outweigh these moral and social factors. The professional full-time working mothers expressed a preference for nursery care on the grounds that it might be better for a child's social development – learning how to socialise and becoming a separate individual. The concerns of African-Caribbean working mothers over formal provision focused on the question of whether their child would face discrimination (which was also a concern voiced by the lesbian mothers interviewed). For this reason they were more likely to use black au pairs, childminders or relatives:

> *'The thing that made me decide on my childminder was that she was a black lady and had lots of experience. With a white childminder it's always in the back of your mind whether they really accept your children.'*

Other research, on fathers, complements Duncan's findings on care/work identities.[6] Being a 'good father' is about being a provider, as well as about 'being there' for your children. But definitions of 'being there' vary from simply being there physically, to spending time, and engaging with the children, to sharing responsibility for childcare more fully. While the distant breadwinner father is no longer the norm, and men have aspirations for a more active involvement in the care of children, constraints still operate, in the organisation of work and in cultural expectations about the proper thing to do as a male provider.

Different trajectories

A subsequent CAVA project by Sarah Irwin focused more closely on the employment practices and values of carers (mainly mothers) of children at primary school.[7] Mothers of pre-school children constitute the group whose employment rates have increased the most over the last 20 years, but the transition of their children to primary school raises particular difficulties given the constraints of school hours and holidays and the needs of small children coping with 'big school'. Irwin was able to unpack the apparent class similarities of middle-class and working-class stay-at-home mothers which Duncan's studies had found. One set of her sample of qualified middle-class mothers either did not work or worked only during school hours on the basis that they had to be there for their children, a view that was echoed by the stay-at-home working-class mothers. However, these two groups revealed quite different trajectories. When asked if they would work full time when the child got older, the qualified middle-class mothers said they would, since the child would be independent enough to cope, while the working-class group said they would stay at home because, as one woman said, 'you still need to spend time with your children whatever age they are'. Different work trajectories influenced the 'proper thing to do' in combining work and care, but they nevertheless found expression in terms of the needs of the child.

Implications for policy and theory

What these research projects show is, first, that there is no single norm of mother/worker or father/worker identity: policy needs to take account of the plurality of balancing acts parents employ, and the different cultures and circumstances that give rise to them. Second, these processes are at odds with the idea that parents will seek to 'make work pay', and that financial inducements to pay for nursery provision will encourage mothers – particularly lone mothers – into paid work. This idea assumes people have a straightforward, instrumental cost–benefit rationality to their decisions about work and care.[8] Costs do come into these decisions – many of the women interviewed by Duncan and his colleagues were working longer hours than they thought was right in order to 'pay the mortgage' – but as far as women were concerned, money was not their primary consideration: women's paid work is valued by them in so far as it enables good mothering to happen. Furthermore, being a mother is not something you do only when you are with your children, nor are mothers transformed into workers only when in employment; rather, 'they [children] sort of occupy so much of your sort of psyche all the time', as Rita, a senior IT consultant put it. Fathers' own work identities are more provider-orientated but 'being there' for the children is also important.

This understanding also throws doubt on some of the overarching claims of the theories about family change in Chapter 1. First, notions of men and women released from fixed gender roles to negotiate more individualised and democratic relationships may be overstated. The death of the male breadwinner may be similarly exaggerated. Gender roles may be less fixed, work/care arrangements more open to negotiation by parents, but they are still underpinned by enduring gender differences and meanings of motherhood and fatherhood. Second, parents' work strategies are influenced by a moral concern for their children's care. This suggests that, instead of focusing on the demoralisation of families and a parenting deficit or work-shyness, concern would be better directed towards providing the *different* sorts of childcare support that parents want and trust, whether formal or informal. However, while respecting the cultures and conditions that influence parents' varying strategies, policies should not reinforce inequalities between them. If black mothers prefer to use black au pairs because they are worried about how their children will be received in a nursery, then the answer is not simply to facilitate the payment of black au pairs but also to introduce more racism-awareness in formal and mainstream provision. Similarly, policies at work to encourage men to take up caring responsibilities in the home should not undermine support for mothers at home or gender equality at work.

Choice and context

Duncan's work, in common with Smart and Neale's research on post-divorce lives, provides an important qualification of the view that both women and men are now much freer to exercise their preferences for either staying at home or going out to work.[9] One should not underestimate the greater freedom that women now have, especially mothers, and especially mothers with qualifications, to take paid work without rebuke. But the research reviewed here shows that the choices they make are not simply a free 'preference' but are embedded in moral considerations and normative ideas about what is right for their children – and that these vary. A counter argument to that of 'free choice' is that mothers' employment choices are constrained by structural factors such as lack of good quality, flexible and affordable childcare; low provision of paid, flexible and adequate caring leave such as maternity leave; shorter working days; and a lack of decently paid jobs. One would not argue with this either, but this view of 'structure' which operates at the level of business and state policy, is refined in Duncan's work to show that local job markets, traditions and cultural networks help shape both the resources available and the moral considerations which influence the choices people make. His research thus offers a much more dynamic picture of agency and structure.

Irwin's research on the parents of primary school children provides an example of this more complex interweaving of local context and 'choice'. She found that people's locality, and their social networks, had a bearing on their patterns of work/care behaviour. Her research was on parents in schools in socially contrasting localities in the Leeds area, including a predominantly white working-class area, a predominantly white middle-class area, and a more disadvantaged area which included both minority ethnic groups and a catchment of middle-class parents. Parents whose children went to one of the primary schools in the predominantly middle-class area favoured combining part-time work with care, whilst at another school in the same area they favoured full-time work. This sort of patterned difference also operated in relation to minority ethnic parents in different schools. In one school black mothers (here mainly mothers of African-Caribbean origin) felt that part-time work or staying at home was the proper thing to do, but in another they opted for full-time work. In other words, peer networks established through local neighbourhood schools had an influence in determining how people weighed their options. The local neighbourhood and school networks act as reference groups in shaping the repertoire of norms and values available to people in working out 'the proper thing to do'.

Mapping local contexts

We can see the significance of local context in a more graphic way through Simon Duncan and Darren Smith's research on the regional and local variations in parenting and partnering forms within the UK.[10] Through national statistical datasets they map the variability of family forms across the country and demonstrate the significance of the local economic, social and cultural context in the social construction of family lives. The main bones of their argument are:

- There is much variability of partnering and parenting patterns across the UK.
- There is no standard 'British family'.
- The 'geography' of family formations does not map onto more familiar explanations of regional differences such as an urban/rural divide, class-based differences or the health of local economies.
- These formations emerge, in part, from the specific nature of the local cultural, economic and social context (as well as being influenced by national/global contexts). The local cultural context – the ideas and assumptions embedded in social networks and local institutions, such as what it means to be a good mother or father and how people ought to behave when they have children – plays a particularly significant part in how people live their family lives and negotiate issues such as the relationship between parenting and paid work. People work out their family lives with reference to locally specific contexts and their everyday social networks, rather than simply with reference to normative ideas and policies that operate at the national level.

These conclusions are demonstrated by Duncan and Smith through their analysis of the spatial nature of family formation patterns, in which they develop four indices. Here we refer to just one of these, the *Motherhood Employment Effect* (MEE; see Map 1, page 64).[11]

The MEE refers to the degree to which women withdraw from full-time employment when they have children. Higher scores represent more women withdrawing from full-time employment to become stay-at-home carers, perhaps with part-time employment fitted around the children's school hours or partners' working hours. Higher scores can therefore be taken as an indicator of the more traditional male breadwinner/female homemaker family form. In contrast, lower scores represent *fewer* women leaving full-time employment following childbirth, and therefore indicate greater adherence to the adult worker model (with dual breadwinners). With this measure, Duncan and Smith are able to capture the impact of having children on a woman's employment position and the domestic division of labour in the household.[12]

What is interesting about Map 1 is that while mothers withdraw from employment after childbirth throughout Britain (unlike in Denmark, for example, where the opposite is true), differences in the degree of withdrawal do not match urban/rural differences, or areas of relative economic prosperity or stagnation, or even class distribution. Thus, in the relatively prosperous South-East of England (outside London), partnered mothers showed a high MEE score (that is, *greater* withdrawal from the labour market at maternity). However, in some areas of relatively stagnant economic fortunes, such as Lancashire or Merseyside, a low MEE score emerges as *fewer* women withdraw from full-time employment. This leads Duncan and Smith to conclude that a mother's employment behaviour is not simply determined by local labour market opportunities, a conclusion which is further supported by the lack of congruence between urban/rural localities and the MEE. Many urban areas, such as Bristol, Hull, Sheffield or Southampton, where, one could argue, women have more access to paid work, demonstrate higher withdrawal rates. However, in other urban contexts, such as Liverpool and Manchester, withdrawal rates are lower with many mothers conforming to the adult worker model. Similarly, some rural areas show high MEEs (as in the West Country) and others show low MEEs (as in much of Wales). These differences also cut across class groups as traditional working-class and middle-class areas may include localities with both high and low MEE scores. Duncan and Smith conclude that this spatial variation in the breadwinner/adult worker model shows two things. First, mothers' withdrawal from full-time work reflects male wages. Where wages are higher and more assured, many women will take up a conventionally defined 'good mother' role – that is, they stay at home with the children (as we have seen, black mothers remain a major exception). Second, this process is about what Duncan and Smith call a 'gender culture' which is marked by differences in locally dominant ideas about the 'proper' relationship between motherhood and paid work.[13] These culturally embedded ideas, built up and reinforced by social networks and everyday interactions, contribute to local patterns of family formation. The historical patterning of women's work – paid and unpaid – in the local area has shaped, and been shaped by, these ideas. The old cotton towns of Lancashire, with some of the lowest MEE scores, are well-known examples, as the earlier illustration of Maxine showed.

The mapping of the geography of family formations confirms what our qualita-

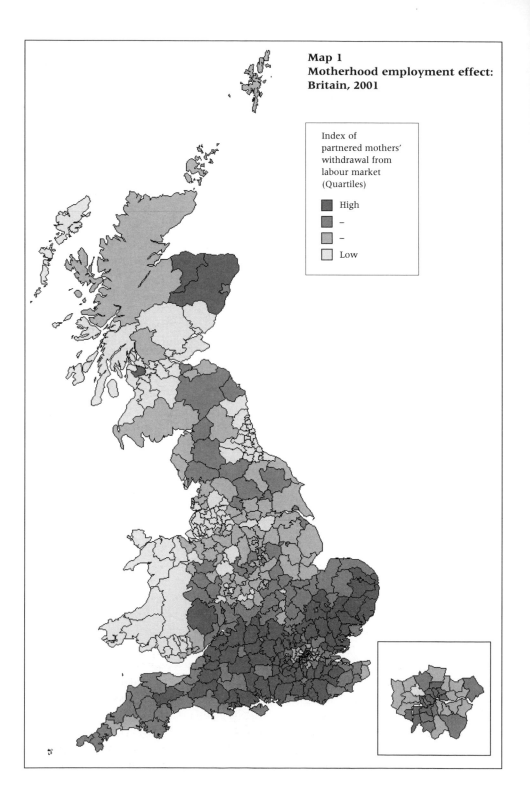

Map 1
Motherhood employment effect:
Britain, 2001

Index of
partnered mothers'
withdrawal from
labour market
(Quartiles)

High
–
–
Low

tive research revealed. The choices mothers make about entering the labour market when they have had a baby are not simply preferences, nor only determined by generalised norms and structures, but are negotiated on the basis of what it means to be a good mother, and this negotiation is influenced by local conditions and social reference groups.

Diversity, culture and change

These CAVA studies on parenting and employment have begun to open up the processes that cause *diversity* in the practices of women and men in balancing work and care responsibilities. In addition, what we can see in this research on work and care, and in the research discussed earlier on divorce, are the complex ways in which both *continuities* and *changes* interweave in people's lives. Gendered caring responsibilities continue, yet negotiation also takes place. However, much that is written about changing family lives appeals to a notion of modernisation which hides these uneven processes of change. Looking at patterns of fertility, cohabitation, marriage, divorce and female employment, Richard Berthoud proposes a continuum of values which places Pakistanis and Bangladeshis at one end (representing 'old-fashioned' values) and whites and African-Caribbeans at the other (representing modern individualism). Although this recognises some of the diversity within ethnic groups, the model tends nevertheless to imply that change moves inexorably in one direction.[14] In another influential argument, David Goodhart proposes that there is 'too much diversity' and this threatens to undermine the 'common culture' and 'moral consensus'. By diversity he means 'a greater diversity in lifestyles and values' to which has been added ethnic diversity through two big waves of immigration – from the Commonwealth countries in the 1950s and 60s and asylum seekers in the 1990s.[15]

Our research shows a more complex process of change than one of laggards and pioneers, or of limitations in the capacity of people to cope with diversity. We find that people acquire the capacity to deal with changes that conflict with their values through weighing up their experiences of, and commitments to, close others. We suggest that this does not detract from a 'common culture'; on the contrary, it adds to the ways in which we are bound to each other – to the mesh of commitment and interdependence – and to the repertoire of competencies that we may draw on to cope with change in our lives. We look at this by returning to some of the research on post-divorce lives discussed earlier.

Conflict and accommodation in coping with divorce
In the study of post-divorce relationships, we noted how grandparents often provided much needed support to their divorced or separated children – especially help with childcare and financial support.[16] Sometimes this served to strengthen existing bonds. At the same time, providing support was not an altogether straightforward process. Many of the grandparents interviewed in this study had married and raised their families when divorce was regarded as both a tragedy and an indication of

moral blame on the part of one or both parties. They felt, at a general level, that the increase in divorce betrayed a loss of moral fibre on the part of people who did not stick at it as they themselves had done. And yet faced with divorce as a reality in their own children's lives, they found it difficult to condemn their children in these blanket terms. The values which guided them through their dilemma were those of commitment and support, of standing by their children in times of trouble; they saw their children's unhappiness and wanted to help. In a way, it reactivated the parent in them, towards both their children and their grandchildren. As one 68-year-old grandfather put it: 'I think you've got to stand by your children. I mean I'm responsible, I'm the one that's brought them into the world or helped to bring them into the world and I'm responsible.' For some, it made them reflect again on their generation's experiences of marriage, of people who had stuck it out and been unhappy, and of family members who faced a lifetime's disapproval for breaking the moral code. In practice, in working out how to be supportive they were prepared to withhold judgement on their children's behaviour. Being non-judgemental was one important way of enabling the relationships after divorce to be maintained.

Divorcing parents, too, often faced a challenge in having previously viewed divorce as something that would never happen to them. When they married they had assumed they were in the relationship for life. In facing the trauma of divorce, many felt they developed new moral competencies in 'doing' relationships. They began to see divorce less as a tragedy, and more as one of life's adversities. Women in particular gained strength from developing a mother identity which was strong, capable and independent. While men might be less affected by the financial insecurity of divorce, finding a new father identity could be harder without the experience of a lot of hands-on fathering. In practice, it was through attentiveness and commitment to the needs of their children that fathers arrived at this, as this father recounts of his initial difficulties:

> 'I invested too much in it and I don't think that was helpful really to Lisa [daughter] in that she had to be too much of a daughter and for Lisa life has got better as I've moved on ... Children are important but they mustn't be too exclusive, bearing in mind that the children concerned have got their own lives to develop and get on with. So they mustn't just be children, they must be children plus friends and everything else and have their own rules in life.'

Parents and grandparents alike faced the dilemmas which resulted from their conflicting values by working out in practice what they felt was the right thing to do for the people they were close to. In articulating to themselves what closeness involved, certain values – such as attentiveness to the needs of others, being non-judgemental, being prepared to be accommodating – emerged as best enabling them to maintain closeness.

Conflict and accommodation in relation to marriage

A second example of culture and change comes from the study on transnational families whose family histories involve the experience of migration to Britain and whose commitments stretch across continents.[17] Smart and Shipman found that in the families of Pakistani and Indian origin that they studied, the 'proper thing to do' when faced with a dilemma over, say, whether an adult child should have an arranged marriage or not, was not simply determined by a set of fixed prescriptions based in Islam or Hinduism, but drew on the value of the commitments they had to the people around them, as well as the context in which they found themselves. When Manju, a Hindu of Indian origin, arrived in Britain from Kenya as a young widow with a son, she felt she could not remarry as this would bring shame on her family abroad. But she also felt that she would be happy for her son to marry out of his caste, or an English girl, in spite of the fact that this too was against her religion, because, given the different context in which he had been brought up, it was important for him to adapt. The researchers found considerable variation in the expectations younger adults had in following an arranged or negotiated marriage. Some felt it was a commitment they owed to family in Pakistan or India. Others felt it was more an individual decision: one mother said she felt that if her children asked her to arrange a partner she would, but equally if they wanted to choose their own she would let them, but she would not want them to marry out of their religion. In so far as arranged marriage is an expression of cultural belonging, some interviewees felt that this belonging could be achieved in other ways, such as by ensuring that their children learned about and became proud of their cultural heritage.

The complexity and unevenness of these negotiations are ignored and made problematic by overarching theories which identify individualisation and freedom to choose as the sole direction of change. Such theories may overstate 'culture' as the driver of change (or, for those who are not going with the flow, as a brake on social change). Culture is not an independent variable; rather, it is a dynamic which shifts and changes over time and place and according to the conditions in which it finds itself. Our research shows that the effects of people's cultural identity, drawn from their generation or from their religion, shape their decisions. But these decisions are also negotiated in and through individual's commitments to others and in their particular contexts.[18] It is unlikely that the moral competencies that people develop and hone in negotiating across cultures – whether these are white British generational cultures or South Asian and British cultures – threaten social cohesion. Far from it; they often strengthen the capacity and resolve of people to attend to the needs of others, to understand and tolerate difference, and to grasp the scope of their own adaptability. To talk of 'too much diversity', as Goodhart does, is to misunderstand the dynamic nature of values shaped by culture, ethnicity and religion.[19] Cultural values do not accumulate, one on top of the other, until there is a surfeit. They adapt themselves to, and are shaped by, the practical ethics of everyday living and close relationships.

Support beyond family and friends

In this chapter we have looked at the effects of work, locality and culture on care and commitments. We now look at the support and reciprocity which rests beyond close friends and family; in this case, the support provided by self-help groups in the community. This was the subject of a further CAVA project carried out by Greg Martin, Sasha Roseneil and Fiona Williams.[20] Their findings begin to link together some of the values which we found were important to care and support *within* family and friends with those values that operate in a less close or intimate context. We were interested in what sorts of parenting and partnering issues were giving rise to self-help organisations which were run *for* and *by* people who had direct experience of a shared concern. This could be having a child with educational or behavioural difficulties, drugs dependency, being a single parent, gay and lesbian parenting, post-natal depression, provision for working parents in rural areas, bereavement, domestic violence, adoption, or divorce and separation. We were also interested in what brought people together and in what they wanted from support.

Shared experiences: protection against stigma

What was common to many of the groups' sense of commitment and reciprocity were feelings of stigma and mis-recognition. Many parents felt they were seen as *bad parents*. This was particularly the case with support groups for parents of children who did not conform to the ideal of being self-responsible, well-behaved and education-oriented; for instance, children with a learning disability such as Attention Deficit Hyperactive Disorder (ADHD). Often parents in this situation experienced isolation and marginalisation; for example, they perhaps shared similar experiences of high-handed treatment by head teachers or doctors. Some groups also felt undermined by discussions of 'social exclusion' which linked their particular experience with other indicators and placed them in a 'social dustbin'. Here, a member of a group for parents whose children have drug dependency problems explains how she got involved:

> 'Once he'd gone in rehab it gave me chance to focus on the problems that I'd gone through as a parent having no support just, you know, suffering on my own because of the stigma, you can't talk to other people about it; the shame, the stigma, you know, the community judges and juries and what have you, you keep it quiet 'cos you feel it's a shame on you, although you've brought your kids up right you feel that you haven't, you know, that's how society makes you feel. Drug addicts are the lowest of the low and the parents must be to blame basically. We all know how it is. So, you know, I suffered for ten years.'[21]

Shared experiences: challenging experts and developing alternative practices

However, shared experience of particular problems was also the basis for challenging what was seen as inappropriate or disrespectful professional practice and knowledge. Becoming an 'expert-by-experience' was one way of claiming the importance of lay knowledge and expertise which professionals often did not have. People said they wanted a more 'holistic' or integrated approach. Also, many groups saw themselves not simply as the receivers and distributors of information but, importantly, through sharing and developing information, as the *providers* of expertise and new knowledge.

The groups often gave their members a sense of belonging and security that was not fully met by family, friends, community or colleagues. The commitments they developed took time to nurture. Nonetheless, it was interesting that what these self-help groups valued in the support they found in each other was not that dissimilar to the practical ethics of care and commitment we found amongst the families and friends we studied. Informality, trust and reciprocity were the key principles in this process. In addition, the need to respect other people's different opinions and experiences and to be non-judgemental was emphasised.

Unwitting exclusion

However, in many cases, this very informality and commitment, often the basis for intense, unique and empowering support, sometimes unwittingly contributed to forms of social exclusion. Most apparent was the lack of involvement of racialised minority ethnic groups in the smaller, more informal and less networked groups. Often white group members had a view that minority ethnic groups preferred to organise on their own and were well supported by their own communities. In contrast, the groups which did focus more specifically on the issues facing minority ethnic parents found they were heavily oversubscribed and overstretched, often because professionals would refer service users to them because they felt they themselves did not have the cultural expertise.[22] However, it was noticeable that when groups became involved in wider networks and put in applications for funding, they were required to look more critically at their own practices of inclusion. The non-involvement of men was also striking,[23] as was the lack of groups for children and siblings.

Fitting into the political agenda

We were further interested in how far such groups were involved at the level of local partnerships and politics and were surprised that many were not. Structures and strategies of local political participation often served to dissipate the efforts of all but the most experienced and networked local activists. Groups which have political roots and are well networked seemed to be more successful, and more aware of how to approach things. It was found that the claims of all local groups were influenced by local political priorities and power. Local and national priorities shape funding opportunities, so that those groups which could fit within a crime and community safety agenda (domestic violence, drugs use) or a health inequalities agenda (teenage pregnancy, exercise and diet) had better access to funds. Small groups often belonged to or supported national voluntary organisations but had no formal way of influencing those organisations, a problem exacerbated by the lack of concentrated focus at the local level on universal (rather than targeted) provision for what have traditionally been called 'family policies'.[24]

The groups emphasised the importance of universal infrastructural provision, especially for childcare, after-school care, transport and counselling. It was within such provision, rather than outside it, that they wanted their specific needs met.

There was also a concern that recent developments focused heavily on the needs of the under-fives so that those with older children felt left out. At the national policy level, the parenting discourse often implies that there is a deficit of parental responsibility. People in these groups were acutely aware of this. Support was very important but, as many groups pointed out, it has to be *the right sort of support* – non-judgemental and non-stigmatising, framed in the values they saw as important (trust, reciprocity, informality and mutual respect), and encompassing the diversity of parenting and partnering experiences. These groups wanted to be valued for the commitments they carry out rather than be made to feel anxious that they are failing, and to be seen as creators of knowledge, information and support rather than as passive receivers of help.

Groups such as these constitute an important net of support for those who fall through the mesh of commitments of family and friends. The relationships and credibility they develop with local communities takes time and long-term commitment deserving of greater financial and political recognition. However, as we argue in the final chapter, the political will that is required to recognise and support the bonds, ties and strands of interdependency is not simply financial or organisational, but about the place of care and commitment in our vision for the future.

Summary

- While there are differences in whether mothers work full time, part time or not at all, some things are held in common. Whether or not they have partners, mothers' decisions are based, first and foremost, on doing *the right thing for their children*. Central to this is their mother/worker identity. Money does matter, but being a 'good mother' matters more.

- Different attitudes to the work/care balance manifest themselves through class, ethnicity, social networks and local traditions and circumstances. Local neighbourhood and school networks act as reference groups in shaping the repertoire of norms and values available to people in making decisions about work and care. The choices they make are not simply free 'preferences' but are embedded in moral considerations and normative ideas about what is right for their children.

- Mothers' different decisions about the sort of childcare options they prefer are similarly influenced by what they feel is right for their child. The *affective* quality of childcare is important, whether it is provided by a relative or a nursery.

- When faced with changes in their close family lives, such as divorce, which challenge their existing values or beliefs, people find ways of coping with the new situation by weighing up how best to sustain commitments to their loved ones. Particular values such as attentiveness to the needs of others, being non-judgemental and being prepared to be accommodating enable people to be resilient to change.

- People juggle with change and continuity in their lives. Cultural and religious influences are important but they are not fixed or the only determinant of people's actions; they are shaped and adapted by the everyday processes of living.

- When people look beyond families and friends for support, self-help groups play an important role, especially where parents feel they fail to match up to normative ideas of responsible parenting. Shared experiences of adversity provide a basis for resisting stigma, for challenging 'expert' knowledge, and for the development of alternative practices of care and support based on reciprocity, trust, mutual respect, informality and being non-judgemental. However, this informality and closeness can unwittingly encourage forms of exclusion, particularly of minority ethnic groups which often lack funding and tend to be outside the participatory processes of local politics.

NOTES

1   Duncan's corpus of research in this area was based on over 260 interviews with lone and partnered mothers from 1993–2001. CAVA's Mothers, Care and Employment project, for which Lise Saugeres interviewed partnered mothers in the CAVA localities, is part of this corpus. For more on this research, see: Duncan and Edwards (1999); Carling, Duncan and Edwards, eds (2002); Duncan (2003); Duncan *et al.* (2003, 2004).
2   Duncan and Edwards (1999), p. 111.
3   Duncan and Edwards (1999), pp. 111–12.
4   Duncan (2003), p. 18. Subsequent quotations are also taken from this paper.
5   See Reynolds, in Carling *et al.*, eds (2002) for a discussion about the variations in parenting and partnering among African-Caribbeans in Britain and some of the 'myths' of cultural heritage.
6   See Hatter, Vintner and Williams (2002). This research divided fathers into occupational sectors. See also O'Brien and Shemilt (2003).
7   See Irwin (2003).
8   Barlow and Duncan (2000a, 2000b).
9   A view expressed by, for example, Hakim (2002).
10 Duncan and Smith (2002).
11 The other indices not shown here are the *Family Conventionality Index*, the *Family Restructuring Index*, and the *Alternative Households Index*.
12 The MEE measure is calculated using 2001 Census data. It compares the full-time employment rate of partnered mothers aged 20–45 years with children against the full-time employment rate of partnered women of the same age group without children. Lone mothers are not included because of their particular position in terms of childcare, income, and partner relations.
13 See also Glucksmann (2000).
14 Berthoud (2000).
15 Goodhart (2004).
16 The discussion here draws on Smart (2003a, 2003c, 2004a, 2004c) and Neale and Smart (2004), and Smart's arguments about a new 'etiquette' for post-divorce lives in Smart (2003c, 2004a). See also Bornat *et al.*, in Harper, ed. (2004).
17 See Smart and Shipman (2004).
18 See also Mason's (2003) paper on burial.
19 This is not to deny that there are some forms of fundamentalism or political racism which are particularly fixed.
20 Williams (2003, 2004a).
21 Williams (2003), p. 9.
22 See also Becher and Hussain (2003).
23 See Williams and Windebank (2000).
24 Proposals in *Every Child Matters* (DfES, 2003) should change this.

5

Rethinking families: rethinking care

This chapter applies our research findings to the values that frame policy. We begin by looking in very general terms at what our findings mean for policy before developing a case for a more radical repositioning of care and commitments in political thinking and strategy.

Doing the 'proper thing'

People's commitments may be different nowadays in that they are less dependent on blood or marriage ties, but, our findings suggest, this does not mean there is a loss of commitment itself. People make morally informed responses to the contexts in which they find themselves. When faced with dilemmas, they draw on repertoires of values about care and commitment in order to work out what, in practice, would be the 'proper thing to do'.

This does not mean everybody is always successful, or acts in the same way. Often, complex negotiations and accommodations are involved which are worked out in and through people's relationships with close others. These are also influenced by a sense of belonging, identity, social networks and local circumstances. There appears to be a general rule that where children are involved their needs should be prioritised.

The decisions people make in their family lives and personal relationships provide little evidence of individuals exercising unencumbered lifestyle choices. People are embedded in relationships that matter to them. There is blurring in these relationships between those that are given and those that are chosen. But we should be cautious about overstating the extent to which individualisation has taken place, or about the extent to which families have broken free of older hierarchies and gendered inequalities. Change has been uneven, and where there has been change it is possible to find continuity too. Nevertheless, aspirations about the quality of relationships, about fairness and mutual respect, and the meaning of people's personal relationships with children, partners, kin and friends are important for their sense of identity and happiness.

Policies that provide time, space and financial security for people to balance their work and care responsibilities and for children to flourish are crucial. Such policies can help break down older inequalities and provide a context in which people can meet care commitments. At a very general level this implies two things for policy:

- First, there should be less anxiety that diverse living arrangements may give rise to moral decline, social instability or lack of social cohesion.
- Second, policies need to focus on practical support for people to carry out their commitments, and to respect and recognise the diversity of these commitments. But it has to be the right sort of support: non-judgemental, fair, respectful and practical.

Pressures for change

It is not just our research findings which provide an argument for a political ethic of care; rather, it is that care, and the context in which care happens, have become central to a wide range of political activities and demands over the last decade.

- The 'care deficit' is central to the welfare reform policies of most European welfare states.
- There are demands around work/life balance from workers and trade unionists coping with longer hours and casualisation.
- There are demands from disability rights and other service users' groups to give users greater say and control over professional care services.
- There is pressure for government strategies on childcare provision and to end child poverty.
- There are now greater demands on parents and their children to ensure educational competence and self-responsible behaviour; increasingly we see prolonged financial dependence of children on their parents.
- There is greater emotional investment by parents in their children as a source of happiness.
- Greater recognition is now given to children's experiences, rights and participation.
- There is more pressure to acknowledge the rights of same-sex partnerships and cohabitees.
- There is also pressure for greater protection and support for adults and children experiencing domestic violence, physical and sexual abuse, and neglect within families and personal relationships.

How people 'do the proper thing'

Our research provides an understanding of the values that act as guidelines for people coping with change and meeting their family and relationship commitments. Moral reasoning based on *care* informs the way people attempt to balance their own sense of self and the needs of others. What it means to be a good mother, father, grandparent, partner, ex-partner, lover, son, daughter or friend is crucial to the way people negotiate the proper thing to do. In working through their dilemmas, certain practical ethics emerge for adults and children, which enable resilience, facilitate commitment and lie at the heart of people's interdependency. They constitute the compassionate realism of 'good-enough' care.[1] They include:

- fairness
- attentiveness to the needs of others
- mutual respect
- trust
- reparation
- being non-judgemental
- adaptability to new identities
- being prepared to be accommodating
- being open to communication.

What is lacking in the current policy debate is a recognition of these ethics and of their importance in people's lives. The emphasis on work overshadows care; interdependency is the poor relation of economic self-sufficiency; and education frames child-centredness. Policies for ensuring children are well educated and their parents are self-sufficient workers have a logic and a laudable aim – of reducing poverty and of enhancing economic competitiveness. However this logic alone does not resonate with what matters to people in their family lives and personal relationships. The practical ethics of fairness, attentiveness and so on cannot simply be transposed into the political arena, but we can use them to develop a wider political ethic of care.

When we interviewed senior representatives from 24 national voluntary organisations who campaign and advise on parenting and partnering issues, the majority looked to an ethos of welfare which emphasises holistic, accessible, affordable user-centred support for parents and children and which places value on care as an activity, on interdependence and on state support to prevent poverty. This ethos is underpinned by notions of social justice which promote anti-discriminatory policies, recognition and respect for diversity, and resistance to widening inequalities. In this the representatives placed special emphasis on valuing care and respecting childhood.[2] We think this ethos reflects and complements the practical ethics which we found in our research on family lives and personal relationships.

Creating an ethic of care

One way of framing these different areas of policy is through a political ethic of care at the heart of which is the aim of *balancing the ethic of work with the ethic of care*. As far as parenting and partnering are concerned, it means redressing the balance of three further elements of current policy:

- Balancing parental responsibilities in favour of supporting parents and listening to them;
- Balancing investment in children with respect for childhood;
- Protecting diversity from inequality.

In Chapter 2 we argue that many of the welfare reforms of New Labour have been based on the centrality of paid work to a conception of citizenship. In particular the ethic of paid work is presented as the central responsibility of citizenship, particularly of parents, in that it offers a route out of dependency into independence and economic self-sufficiency, as well as a role model to children. It has been developed as the solution to poverty and the condition of eligibility to tax credits for family support. Paid work is also seen as the interface between individuals and the wider society and the glue that binds society together.

Paid work is undeniably important in terms of a sense of self. Women and disabled people fought for the right to equal access to the labour market. But the ethic of paid work is not a broad enough principle to meet the aspirations which people have around time and the quality of their relationships. What is needed is a political principle about care which is equivalent to that about paid work. Only if care and work are linked together can we argue for and defend the disparate measures that have been taken, and those that need to be developed.

We would propose that the ethic of care be seen as the basis of citizenship, social cohesion, and the promotion of equality. The core of this argument is that:

- Where the work ethic elevates the notion of independence and economic self-sufficiency, an ethic of care demands that *interdependence* be seen as the basis of human interaction; it is people's connectedness to each other, and their expectation of recognition from others, that inform their actions.[3] This does not deny the importance of autonomy: autonomy and independence are about the capacity for self-determination rather than simply an expectation of individual self-sufficiency.
- Care, of both oneself and others, is meaningful activity in its own right. It is also universal; we are all, at some level and at some point, the givers and receivers of care from others. Vulnerability is a fundamental human condition and we are all more or less vulnerable than others at different times and in different places. Care is not an activity exclusive to women, but only by giving it public validation as a social good can it be presented as complementary to the 'male breadwinner' model for men and boys.

- In providing and receiving care and support in conditions of mutual respect we learn and enact the practical ethics of being attentive to others: responsibility, trust, being adaptable and accommodating to others' differences, toleration for our own and others' human frailty, and how to sustain and repair relationships. These are not just personal qualities, but contribute to social cohesion. They can be seen as civic virtues and therefore as part of what it means to be a citizen.[4] Care is part of citizenship.

Dilemmas of care

Care and caring relationships can also give rise to inequalities, abuses of power and forms of unwanted dependency. These operate on three levels. Those who take on the responsibility of providing unpaid care may well find their own access to an independent income is diminished. Those who are cared for find themselves in a position of double dependency; and, when care as an activity remains undervalued, the position of those who provide paid care is also usually low-paid and regarded as unskilled.

In seeking to promote and value care we must also consider the possibility that we are simply reinforcing these inequalities and, in particular, the gendered divisions between men and women. Our interviews with mothers about their work/care and childcare preferences revealed that many felt that their place was with their children, particularly while they were young, and many preferred to use care they could trust such as partners or female relatives, rather than formal nursery care provision. In respecting this diversity by, for example, providing a care-giver payment to a parent or chosen relative we may be reinforcing the inequalities that result from mothers' long-term withdrawal from the labour market. We may also reinforce the idea that it is women's place to care, and men's place to be in the labour market. In addition, encouraging the home-based care of three- to five-year-olds may not always be in all children's best interests. Children, like adults, enjoy and benefit from relationships with other children and adults.

On the other hand, policies that encourage men and women to become independent earners – without adequately addressing issues of 'who cares' run the risk of amplifying existing inequalities in the workplace, not only between men and women, but between women in terms of socio-economic status, educational qualifications and whether they have access to a partner's wage. It is against this background that we make the following recommendations to policy-makers.

Promoting an ethic of care

Time to care
In researching the question of how mothers make decisions about combining paid work and care (see Chapter 4), we found that their moral reasoning was based on

their understanding of what makes a good mother and how that fitted into work, more than about the financial rewards that paid work could bring. With policies and political debates that increasingly stress parental responsibilities, and with work trends which increase the demands placed on workers, parents are left in the difficult position of having to decide how to resolve these pressures. Appeals to mothers to take up paid employment on the basis of the ethic of work may well fail to hit the mark, whereas policies and reasoning based on the ethic of care are more likely to find favour.

If work/life balance is actually to *mean* balance, then instead of paid work being the starting point and the question being how, as a society, we are to fit our life around our paid work, we put it the other way round and ask: how do we fit our work around our life? Balancing these two ethics, of work and care, enables us to think about how we organise time and our environment – our space – differently. Rather than care needs being fitted in with the traditional requirements of work, we can start by asking what is important for the following areas of our lives:

- *Care of others:* what do we need to meet our commitments to provide proper care and support for close kin and friends?
- *Care of the self:* what do we need in terms of time and space for the maintenance of body, mind and soul? Much of the focus of debates on the work/life balance is about providing time for care responsibilities, but ignores time for self-development and reflection. Similarly, care policies for people who require greater support focus on this need for support rather than balancing it with their need for self-determination.
- *Care of the world:* what support do we need to be able to have a say, to contribute to and to participate in our communities?
- *Work time and space:* what do we need to enable us to gain economic self-sufficiency and to balance these other areas?

The structures that would enable people to achieve this work/life balance would include:

- Provision of services such as childcare, home care services, cleaning, laundry, food services, domiciliary services, and residential services, underpinned by principles of accessibility, affordability, variety, choice, quality, flexibility, and user control;
- Removal of disabling barriers around space, time, organisations and the environment and a commitment to a caring, enabling environment – safe and accessible public spaces with safe, accessible, and affordable transport;
- Local strategies which integrate issues of work, time, care, space and welfare services, such as the 'Time in the City' projects in Modena, Italy. Here, trade unions, local authorities and employers have collaborated to establish how best to schedule the working time of public and commercial organisations to fit in with the needs of those who use them, and also to work out how this could be

effected in order to give those who work in these services greater flexibility in their working times. This was combined with developing a network of nurseries and eldercare facilities;

- Developing 'care' cultures in work, and also in social and political organisations – such as Parliament, the trade unions, and welfare services – in order to move away from the male breadwinner model and culture and to emphasise the relational aspects of people's lives.

Care as work

One of the effects of women's working and of increased longevity is the greater demand for household services – in childcare, eldercare, domestic cleaning, home maintenance and food services – and it is likely this demand will increase. But the working conditions and pay for such work are poor,[5] and for those working outside the state and the voluntary sectors, there is little social protection. Much of the work is cash-in-hand and done by women. Career prospects are limited because there is no formal route into this type of work, no career progression and the expertise and skills required go unrecognised.[6] At the same time, the supply of workers going into care work is drying up. Some countries depend on migrant workers to fill the gaps and this can be particularly exploitative.[7] On the other hand, user groups such as the disability rights movement have argued that formal training and professionalisation tend to produce people with a pathological model of disability. Strategies to deal with these tensions would involve:

- Establishing and formalising career paths into the household service sector;
- Developing training for care work that is person-centred rather than task-oriented and based on the practical ethics of everyday life that we outlined earlier (e.g. being attentive to people's needs, being non-judgemental; recognising human dignity); and a much greater involvement of user groups in monitoring courses and trainees;
- Developing accreditation frameworks that recognise experience acquired from the job.

Supporting care

The research we carried out suggested that many of the people we interviewed felt their responsibilities as parents and children very keenly. Many of those who were involved in self-help groups felt stigmatised by being a parent of a child with particular difficulties or by themselves having a condition which meant that their parenting capacity was reduced. Similarly, many divorced parents interviewed had absorbed ideas of divorce as a social problem and felt very much responsible for the consequences. At the same time, parents often shied away from formal support. Many in the self-help groups had gone along to or started a group because of negative experiences of head teachers, of social services, or health care organisations. In Britain, state intervention for parents has been seen as reserved for the poor or pathological. Mistrust between statutory agencies, parents and children is not uncommon; at the root of this mistrust is a fear of the power of the state to take children into care, combined with a sense of devaluation of the efforts that many parents make, albeit in diverse ways, to live up to their aspirations of being good and responsible parents. Policies for parents seem to weigh heavily in favour of statutory intervention which reinforces and monitors parental responsibilities, and far less in terms of providing for parental participation and support.[8]

Tony Blair has promised that his government 'will not hesitate to encourage and even enforce' the obligation 'to bring up children as competent, responsible citizens and to support those – such as teachers – who are employed by the state in the task'.[9] In these terms, the government envisages support as conditional upon the carrying out of responsibilities. Our research indicates that it may be wise to prioritise measures to engender trust from parents first:

- Parents want access to support, but it has to be *the right sort of support*; the wrong sort of help can be damaging to people's self-esteem and their capacity for involvement with others.[10] The support parents offer each other in self-help groups is often based on informality, reciprocity, mutual respect, and non-judgemental commitment which has taken time to build up, and it is this support they trust.
- Much greater emphasis needs to be given to strategies to build stronger local communities and local democracy. The research on mothers and employment has shown how local cultures and networks influence the way people think about their childcare strategies. Local, rooted, community and self-help groups lack stable funding, yet they often provide parents and children with the support they require. The relationships and credibility such groups develop with local communities take time and long-term commitment, which needs much greater recognition. Community-based workers, paid and unpaid, are extremely over-stretched, especially those who facilitate minority ethnic groups.
- Where possibilities exist for local participation, our research showed that local support groups had little control of the overall agenda. Attempts to get funding had to fit around priorities such as crime and safety that are set by central government. Current proposals to base services in schools will help reduce stigma but may deter those whose relationship with schools is already difficult.
- New Labour has taken some important steps to reduce child poverty and to develop Sure Start initiatives in selected areas. Further strategies for community-based services and for invigorating communities need also to be tied more clearly to anti-poverty strategies for children and their families.[11]

Rights and fairness

The assumption of a simple equation of rights and responsibilities does not work well with questions of care. Smart and Neale argue, for example, that the assumption of rights for parents and children is too rigid a measure to follow when courts are dealing with the care of children following divorce.[12] They suggest, on the basis of their research into the experience of parents and children at divorce, that such decisions require the following mediating principles deriving from an ethic of care:

- *Actuality*: recognises the importance of making decisions with reference to the reality of the lives involved. Whether, for example, any family members have been subject to violence would weigh more heavily than the principle that shared care after divorce is in the child's best interests;
- *Care*: would consider the care needs of the child in terms of the quality of relationships the child has with his or her parents and how these might be fostered over time;
- *Recognition of selfhood and of loss*: parents' immediate post-divorce experiences often involve a loss of confidence and a need to build up their sense of who they are. Becoming a non-resident parent also causes feelings of loss and grief and acknowledging these is important to facilitate a less conflictual process.

This does not discard notions of justice and rights but focuses on the practical ethics which ensure fairness for all concerned. In our interviews with national voluntary organisations who lobby about parenting and partnering issues, one representative of a children's charity explained how difficult ideas of 'rights' can be in family processes:

> *'I think it goes back to a fundamental question of what is the family like, is the family a sort of hierarchy or democracy I suppose is what it comes down to. And what are rights for? ... I'm against using the word "rights" because I think it's a gift to the various lobbies that are around children's rights and parents' rights, and that's why I would go more back to the good childhood and what part we play as adults in helping children to reach their potential. I'd frame it around that.'*[13]

Respecting and investing

Investing in children as our future has been the theme of much-needed recent early years education and childcare strategies for young children. As Gordon Brown, the Chancellor, has said: 'Nothing is more important to the future of our whole country than that, with the best schooling, services and financial support, every child has the chance to develop their potential.'[14] The 2003 Green Paper *Every Child Matters*, which supported the setting up of a Ministry for Children, Young People and Families, goes a long way in setting out structures of accountability to protect children, to recognise their needs and to create educational opportunities to enable them to become productive future citizens.[15] But while it is strong on protection and recognition of needs, especially for educational achievement, the emphasis seems to be more about supporting the processes of *becoming an adult* than fostering the active enjoyment and negotiation of childhood and young personhood with friends and siblings. The Green Paper has less to say about creating a culture of *respect* for children and childhood, which would be part and parcel of an ethic of care. In addition, the argument for *investing* in children provides little rationale for attending to the needs of those who may not have an educational future – older people, disabled people and children with learning disabilities. Our research on self-help groups found that it was parents of children with learning disabilities who felt most marginalised by developments in policy. These parents felt failures because they could not easily combine the care of their children with work, and because they were not producing self-responsible children with qualifications. Where these parents and their children are also members of minority ethnic groups, the lack of formal or informal support was even more evident. Respecting children and childhood would involve:

- Listening to what children say and respecting them as citizens of the present and not just of the future. The Joseph Rowntree Foundation's Report *Citizenship for Young Children* develops a framework and strategies for the involvement not only of young people but also of young children in nurseries, schools and public services.[16] Its strategies focus on children as creative human actors and involve them in running their nurseries and primary schools, helping staff to develop criteria for recruitment, contributing to training, and training children in articulating their needs and making their claims. The Report argues that such processes should be part of the routine experiences of children, and regarded as a vital part of recognising and developing their capabilities and right to flourish. Such strategies identify education as a site for children's enjoyment of their social relationships and for creativity in order to enhance self-esteem, whatever their educational potential, as well as a place for gaining qualifications.[17]
- Providing opportunities for involvement in local communities. Research on teenage boys has shown that they are acutely aware of being seen as socially and educationally problematic, of being disparaged by adults in their lives and, as a consquence, they continually demand greater respect.[18] Small-group discussion spaces for boys in schools with adults skilled in listening are important. This would be in line with recent initiatives and pilot schemes in 'emotional literacy' in schools, and could foster the emotional capacity of boys as future carers and fathers, and not simply their educational qualifications as future workers.[19]
- Giving children a voice in both social and private areas of their lives. The research on children's experiences of divorce in Chapter 3 showed how the notion of 'the child's best interests' has meaning only if children themselves are given the space to communicate what they feel this is. Notions of fairness sometimes dealt only with fairness between parents rather than including children. It was suggested that parents and other adults involved in the divorce process needed to heed children's views on fairness, care, respect and trust.
- Respecting the childhood of troubled and troublesome children. Current policies in Britain have failed so far to respond to demands to increase the age of criminal responsibility from 10 to 12, and to end the use of custodial sentences for 12- to 14-year-olds, particularly when they have not been persistent offenders. The commitment, under pressure from children's organisations, to withdraw parents'

rights to physical chastisement of their children is welcomed. However, an anti-smacking culture can flourish only in a climate where parents feel they them-selves are trusted and respected and can pass these sentiments on to their children.

Protecting diversity from inequality

Our findings reveal also that moves to recognise diversity may sometimes expose or reinforce inequality. We have already noted that moves to recognise carers should not have the effect of making women less equal in the workplace. Another example is in the proposal for civil partnerships which extends most of the rights associated with heterosexual marriage to same-sex relationships. However, this still leaves heterosexual cohabitees unprotected in relation to legal rights. Extending social secu-rity and taxation policy to all couples strengthens the notion of the sexual couple as the basic unit for entitlements, but fails to recognise different kinds of close commit-ments based on friendship or relationships not involving cohabitation. Policy, both in its everyday practices and also in its rights and entitlements, may have to take on board people's own definitions of closeness and commitment.[20]

Creating special support services for minority ethnic people can result in greater inequality where people are given low priority within mainstream programmes.[21] For example, African-Caribbean mothers are reluctant to use childcare services which are not alert to children's experiences of racism. This calls for culture- and racism-awareness in such services. Ensuring that diversity does not equal inequality means attending to the specifics of what is now called 'institutional racism' in main-stream services, along with both greater resourcing and involvement of local groups and a properly informed and non-judgemental cultural sensitivity. In this respect, cultural awareness involves an understanding not only of the different value systems of different faiths and ethnicities, but how, for individuals, these systems operate not as fixed rules but according to the contexts in which they live.

Conclusion

'Above all, we need a vision which places a value on people's care, their commitments, and caring activities.'

Our research has investigated how people in contemporary Britain negotiate their family lives and personal relationships under new conditions of divorce and re-partnering, cohabitation, working and caring, and kin-keeping at a distance. We have found that while these new conditions may have changed the shape of commitments they have not undermined commitment itself. It is their relationships with close others, rather than self-interest, that generally guide people in deciding 'the proper thing to do'. In dealing with their dilemmas people do not refer to abstract moral principles, but work out what to do in practice and in context, according to the needs of others and the significance and history of their close relationships.

We found that the ethics that enabled people to be resilient included fairness, attentiveness to the needs of others, mutual respect, trust, reparation, being non-judgemental, adaptability to new identities, being prepared to be accommodating, and being open to communication. Respect, trust and being non-judgemental were also what people wanted when they sought support beyond friends and family. It is through relationships with other adults and with their children that people strive to give their lives shape, meaning and satisfaction. The choices that people make in their lives are not simply individual choices or preferences but are influenced by their relationships with others, social networks and local circumstances.

Using the evidence from our research we have argued in this chapter that the significance that people attach to care and commitment in their lives is underestimated by policy-makers in three ways. First, it is often assumed that contemporary social change means that people have lost their sense of moral values or that they are too self-interested to understand the meaning of commitment. Second, much of the caring activity that happens is taken for granted, made invisible and not valued. Third, policies are often based on an assumption that people are motivated by the financial advantages that paid work brings, rather than by the commitments they have to others. Money matters, but parents and partners balance its importance with the quality of care they feel they can best offer their children and their own understanding of what it means to be a good mother or father, partner or friend. We have therefore argued that an ethic of care based on the significance of people's care commitments, and the contribution these make to citizenship, would find greater support in developing policies than arguments based on the work ethic alone.

Balancing acts
In the short term, we have suggested four rebalancing acts:

- to balance the ethic of work with the ethic of care;
- to support parents' responsibilities by listening to what they need;
- to balance investment in children with respect for childhood;
- to protect diversity from inequality.

Policies should be neither prescriptive nor uniform but flexible enough to support people in the contexts in which they find themselves and the commitments they have. They should seek to develop much greater democratic, local involvement of children and adults in the services they want. They should encourage public dialogue on work and care, informed by the different views and experiences of adults and children.

The longer term
The longer term is about the direction that we should take given how families and personal relationships are changing. Above all, we need a vision which places a value

on people's care, their commitments, and caring activities. It is in these terms that we have talked about the importance of a political ethic of care which can link together strategies in the workplace, strategies to encourage the sharing of care in the home for men and women, and strategies to support care in local communities and to respect care practices within and between families and friends. This would see care as part of citizenship, and as contributing to a more egalitarian, inclusive, inter-dependent and cohesive society. It would begin, in the twenty-first century, to rebal-ance the twentieth-century fixation on the ethic of work.

Summary

The practical ethics of good-enough care that emerge from our research findings have important implications for social policies. Crucially, they point to a case for a more radical repositioning of care in political think-ing and strategy that will resonate with what matters to people in their family lives and personal relationships. We have called this an ethic of care. It involves:

- **Balancing the work ethic with the care ethic**. We start with the question: how do we best support each other? We argue that the care ethic recognises that care is universal and that it emphasises inter-dependency, acknowledges vulnerability, and encourages trust and tolerance; these are important civic virtues that sustain social cohesion. An ethic of care rejects the inequalities and unwanted forms of depend-ency that arise from the devaluation of caring activities in society.

- **Making time to care.** We need support for flexible working hours and conditions, access to affordable good-quality care provision, a framework of financial support for parents and carers, and better pay and conditions and training for care workers, so that men and women are able to choose how they combine work and care. But we also have to think innova-tively about the reorganisation of time and space in order to meet people's expectations of how to care properly for others, for themselves and for the communities in which they live.

- **Supporting parents and listening to them**. The notion of 'no rights without responsibilities' is out of touch with the moral basis of people's commitments and with the sense of responsibility that is keenly felt by them. Values of fairness, respect, trust and care are more appropriate. Government needs to overcome mistrust and provide support that respects, is non-judgemental and practical, and gives its users a voice.

- **Recognising that investment in care is for the present, not just the future**. Current policies for children are framed in terms of the con-tribution they will make to society in the future. This way of thinking eclipses a view of children as citizens of the present with voices to be heard, nor does it address the present needs of disabled and older people. A wider 'joined up' framing of care in terms of respect for those we care for recognises creativity, sociability and emotional competence in all those who are cared for and does not simply expect a dividend from them in terms of, for example, educational success and good behaviour.

- **Protecting diversity from inequalities**. Policies based on the ethic of care should recognise and value care, but must not reinforce differences and inequalities between men and women or between different communities or localities. Policies need to be diverse and flexible enough to meet people's varying options for their living arrangements and for combining work and care in the short term. They also have to be part of a longer-term vision that attends to the complex inequalities and hierarchies that are part of current caring practices between men and women, adults and children, and carers and cared-for.

NOTES

1 The child psychoanalyst Donald Winnicott in the 1950s used the term 'good-enough mothering' to describe the care that was sufficient to provide a basis for the subjectivity of an infant to develop. See Froggett (2002) for a discussion; and also Smart and Silva, eds (1999); Smart and Neale (1997); Williams (1999).
2 See the 'Collective Voices' project in Appendix 2, and also Roseneil and Williams, 2004.
3 See Honneth (1996).
4 See Tronto (1993); Sevenhuijsen,(1999); Williams (2001).
5 Cancedda, ed. (2001); Ungerson (2003); Yeandle (1999).
6 Toynbee (2003).
7 Anderson (2000); Ungerson (2003); Williams, in Knijn and Komter, eds (2004b).
8 DfES (2003).
9 Tony Blair in 1998, quoted in Deacon (2004).

10 Ghate and Hazel (2002); Williams (2003).
11 UK Coalition Against Poverty (2000).
12 Smart and Neale, (1999) pp. 192–7.
13 Roseneil and Williams (2004).
14 Gordon Brown, quoted in Curphey (2003), p. 19.
15 See Williams (2004c).
16 Neale (2003). See also Moss and Petrie (2002).
17 Room 13 in Caol Primary School in Fort William has been spectacularly successful. It is an art studio run *by* children, *for* children. It produces outstanding art work from 'ordinary' children and enhances co-operation, self-esteem and knowledge. For more information, see their website: www.room13scotland.com.
18 Frosh, Phoenix and Pattman (2002).
19 See www.w-lb.org.uk.
20 Barlow *et al.*, in Park *et al.*, eds (2002); Roseneil and Budgeon (2004).
21 Becher and Hussain (2003).

Bibliography

L. Ackers, 'From "Best Interests" to Participatory Rights: Children's Involvement in Family Migration Decisions', Working Paper Series 18 (University of Leeds, Centre for Research on the Family, Kinship and Childhood, 2000).

L. Alanen and B. Mayall, *Conceptualising Child-Adult Relations* (London, Routledge/Falmer, 2001).

B. Anderson, *Doing the Dirty Work? The Global Politics of Domestic Labour* (London, Z Books, 2000).

C. Attwood, G. Singh, D. Prime, R. Creasey and others, *2001 Home Office Citizenship Survey: People, Families and Communities*, Home Office Research Study 270 (London, Development and Statistics Directorate, Home Office, 2003).

A. Barlow and S. Duncan, 'Supporting Families? New Labour's Communitarianism and the "Rationality Mistake": Part 1', *Journal of Social Welfare and Family Law*, 22 (1), 2000a, pp. 23–42.

A. Barlow and S. Duncan, 'New Labour's Communitarianism, Supporting Families and the "Rationality Mistake": Part 2', *Journal of Social Welfare and Family Law*, 22 (2) 2000b, pp. 129–43.

A. Barlow, S. Duncan, G. James and A. Park, 'Just a Piece of Paper? Marriage and Cohabitation in the UK', in A. Park, J. Curtice, K. Thomson, L. Jarvis, and C. Bromley, eds, *British Social Attitudes: The 19th Report* (London, Sage in association with the National Centre for Social Research, 2002).

A. Barlow and G. James, 'Regulating Marriage and Cohabitation in 21st Century Britain', *Modern Law Review*, 67 (2), 2004, pp. 144–76.

Z. Bauman, *Liquid Love: On the Frailty of Human Bonds* (Cambridge, Polity Press, 2003).

H. Becher and F. Hussain, *Supporting Minority Ethnic Families: South Asian Hindus and Muslims in Britain: Developments in Family Support* (London, National Family and Parenting Institute, 2003).

U. Beck and E. Beck-Gernsheim, *The Normal Chaos of Love* (Cambridge, Polity Press, 1995).

U. Beck and E. Beck-Gernsheim, *Individualization: Institutionalized Individualism and its Social and Political Consequences* (London, Sage, 2002).

G.S. Becker, *An Economic Analysis of the Family* (Dublin, Economic and Social Research Institute, 1986).

G.S. Becker, *A Treatise on the Family* (Cambridge, Harvard University Press, 1991).

A. Bennett, *Telling Tales* (London, BBC Worldwide Limited, 2000).

B. Bernstein and J. Brannen, *Children, Research and Policy* (London, Taylor Francis, 1996).

R. Berthoud, 'Family Formation in Multi-Cultural Britain: Three Patterns of Diversity', Institute for Social and Economic Research Working Paper 34 (Colchester, University of Essex, 2000).

J. Bornat, B. Dimmock, D. Jones and S. Peace, 'Intergenerational Relationships among UK Stepfamilies', in S. Harper, ed., *Families in Ageing Societies – A Multi-Disciplinary Approach* (Oxford, Oxford University Press, 2004).

J. Bradshaw, 'Child Poverty and Child Outcomes', *Children and Society*, 16 (2), 2002, pp. 131–40.

A. Broomfield, *All Our Children Belong: Exploring the Experiences of Black and Minority Ethnic Parents of Disabled Children* (London, Parents for Inclusion, 2004).

C. Bryson, T. Budd, J. Lewis and G. Elam, *Women's Attitudes to Combining Paid Work and Family Life* (London, HMSO, The Cabinet Office, 2000).

A. Cancedda, ed., *Employment and Household Services* (Dublin, European Foundation for the Improvement of Living and Working Conditions, 2001).

A. Carling, S. Duncan and R. Edwards, eds, *Analysing Families: Morality and Rationality in Policy and Practice* (London, Routledge, 2002).

K. Chahal, *Racist Harassment Support Projects: Their Role, Impact and Potential* (York, York Publishing Services in association with the Joseph Rowntree Foundation, 2003).

K. Chahal and L. Julienne, *'We can't all be White!' Racist Victimisation in the UK* (York, York Publishing Services in association with the Joseph Rowntree Foundation, 1999).

M. Chamberlain, ed., *Caribbean Migration: Globalised Identities* (London, Routledge, 1998).

M. Cockett and J. Tripp, *The Exeter Family Study: Family Breakdown and its Impact on Children* (Exeter, University of Exeter Press, 1994).

R. Crompton, M. Brockmann and R.D. Wiggins, 'A Woman's Place ... Employment and Family Life for Men and Women', in A. Park, J. Curtice, K. Thomson, L. Jarvis and C. Bromley, eds, *British Social Attitudes: The 20th Report* (London, Sage in association with the National Centre for Social Research, 2003).

M. Curphey, 'The Parents' Trap', *The Guardian*, 10 December 2003.

R. Dahlberg, P. Moss and A. Pence, *Beyond Quality in Early Childhood Education and Care: Some Perspectives* (London, Falmer Press, 1999).

Daycare Trust, *Parent's Eye: Building a Vision of Equality and Inclusion in Childcare Services* (London, Daycare Trust, 2003).

A. Deacon, *(Re)thinking the Unthinkable: Conditionality, Equality and Welfare* (London, Social Market Foundation, 2004, in press).

S. Dench, J. Aston, C. Evans, N. Meager, M. Williams, R. Willison, *Key Indicators of Women's Position in Britain* (London, Department of Trade and Industry, Women and Equality Unit, 2002).

N. Dennis and G. Erdos, *Families without Fatherhood*, second edn (London, Institute for the Study of Civil Society, 1993).

Department for Education and Skills (DfES), *Every Child Matters* (London, HMSO, 2003).

Department of Work and Pensions (DWP), *Family Resources Survey 2000–2001* (London, HMSO, 2003).

S. Dex, *Families and Work in the Twenty-First Century* (York, Joseph Rowntree Foundation, 2003).

B. Dobson, S. Middleton and A. Beardsworth, *The Impact of a Childhood Disability on Family Life* (York, York Publishing Services in association with the Joseph Rowntree Foundation, 2001).

S. Duncan, 'Mothers, Care and Employment: Values and Theories', CAVA Working Paper 1 (Leeds, CAVA, 2003), www.leeds.ac.uk/cava/papers/workingpapers

S. Duncan and R. Edwards, *Lone Mothers, Paid Work and Gendered Moral Rationalities* (Basingstoke, Macmillan, 1999).

S. Duncan, R. Edwards, T. Reynolds and P. Alldred, 'Motherhood, Paid Work and Parenting: Values and Theories', *Work, Employment and Society*, 17 (2), 2003, pp. 309–30.

S. Duncan, R. Edwards, T. Reynolds and P. Alldred, 'Mothers and Child Care: Policies, Values and Theories', *Children and Society*, 18 (4), 2004, in press.

S. Duncan and D. Smith, 'Geographies of Family Formations: Spatial Differences and Gender Cultures in Britain', *Transactions of the Institute of British Geographers*, 27, 2002, pp. 471–93.

S. Duncan and M. Strell, 'Combining Lone Motherhood and Paid Work: The Rationality Mistake and Norwegian Social Policy', *Journal of European Social Policy*, 14 (1), 2004, pp. 55–69.

S. Duncan and F. Williams, eds, 'New Divisions of Labour?', *Critical Social Policy*, 22 (1), 2002.

G.A. Dunne, 'A Passion for "Sameness": Sexuality and Gender Accountability', in E.B. Silva and C. Smart, eds, *The New Family: The New Practices and Politics of Family Life* (London, Sage, 1999).

J. Ermisch and M. Francesconi, 'The Increasing Complexity of Family Relationships: Lifetime Experience of Lone Motherhood and Stepfamilies in Great Britain', *European Journal of Population*, 16 (3), 2000, pp. 235–49.

A. Etzioni, *The Parenting Deficit* (London, Demos, 1993).

Eurostat, *The European Labour Force Survey 2003* (Luxembourg, Statistical Office of the European Communities, 2004a).

Eurostat, *People and Households Database* (Luxembourg, Statistical Office of the European Communities, 2004b).

E. Ferri, J. Bynner and M. Wadsworth, eds, *Changing Britain, Changing Lives: Three Generations at the Turn of the Century*, The Bedford Way Series (University of London, Institute of Education, 2003).

R. Fevre, *The Demoralization of Western Culture: Social Theory and the Dilemmas of Modern Living* (London, Continuum, 2000).

G. Fimister, ed., *An End in Sight? Tackling Child Poverty in the UK* (London, Child Poverty Action Group, 2001).

J. Finch, *Family Obligations and Social Change* (Cambridge, Polity Press, 1989).

J. Finch and J. Mason, *Negotiating Family Responsibilities* (London, Tavistock/Routledge, 1993).

J. Flowerdew and B. Neale, 'Children with Multiple Challenges in their Post Divorce Family Lives', Working Paper 29 (University of Leeds, Centre for Research on Family, Kinship and Childhood, 2003).

L. Froggett, *Love, Hate and Welfare: Psychosocial Approaches to Policy and Practice* (Cambridge, Polity Press, 2002).

S. Frosh, A. Phoenix and R. Pattman, *Young Masculinities: Understanding Boys in Contemporary Society* (Basingstoke, Palgrave, 2002).

D. Ghate and N. Hazel, *Parenting in Poor Neighbourhoods: Stress, Support and Coping* (London, Jessica Kingsley, 2002).

A. Giddens, *Modernity and Self-Identity: Self and Society in the Late Modern Age* (Cambridge, Polity Press, 1991).

A. Giddens, *The Transformation of Intimacy: Sexuality, Love and Eroticism in Modern Societies* (Cambridge, Polity Press in association with Basil Blackwell, 1992).

A. Giddens, *The Third Way: The Renewal of Social Democracy* (Cambridge, Polity Press, 1999).

V. Gillies, J. Ribbens-McCarthy and J. Holland, *'Pulling Together, Pulling Apart': The Family Lives of Young People* (London, Family Policy Studies Centre in association with the Joseph Rowntree Foundation, 2001).

J.R. Gillis, 'Virtual Families: A Cultural Approach', Working Paper 28 (University of Leeds, Centre for Research on Family, Kinship and Childhood, 2003).

D. Gittens, *The Family in Question: Changing Households and Familiar Ideologies*, second edn (Basingstoke, Macmillan, 1993).

M. Glucksmann, *Cottons and Casuals: The Gendered Organisation of Labour in Time and Space* (Durham, Sociology Press, 2000).

D. Goodhart, 'Too Diverse?', *Prospect Magazine*, 95, February 2004 [web version].

A. Gray, 'Making Work Pay: Devising the Best Strategy for Lone Parents in Britain', *Journal of Social Policy*, 30 (2), 2001, pp. 189–207.

C. Hakim, *Models of the Family in Modern Societies: Ideals and Realities* (Aldershot, Ashgate, 2002).

W. Hatter, L. Vintner and R. Williams, *Dads on Dads: Needs and Expectations at Home and Work* (Manchester, Equal Opportunities Commission, 2002).

S. Heath, 'Peer-Shared Households, Quasi-Communities and Neo-Tribes', *Current Sociology*, 52 (2), 2004, pp. 161–79.

E.M. Hetherington, 'Social Support and the Adjustment of Children in Divorced and Remarried Families', *Childhood*, 10 (2), 2003, pp. 217–36.

B. Hobson, 'The Individualised Worker, the Gender Participatory and the Gender Equity Models in Sweden', *Social Policy and Society*, 3 (1), 2004, pp. 75–83.

Home Office, *Supporting Families: A Consultation Document* (London, HMSO, 1998).

Home Office, *British Crime Survey 2000* (London, HMSO, 2000).

Home Office, *Safety and Justice: The Government's Proposals for Domestic Violence* (London, HMSO, 2003).

House of Commons Work and Pensions Committee, *Childcare for Working Parents: Fifth Report of Sessions 2002–3, Volume 1* (London, HMSO, 2003).

A. Honneth, *Struggle for Recognition: The Moral Grammar of Social Conflicts* (Cambridge, Polity Press, 1996).

J. Huber and P. Skidmore, *The New Old: Why Baby Boomers won't be Pensioned Off* (London, Demos, 2003).

F. Hussain and M. O'Brien, 'Muslim Communities in Europe: Reconstruction and Transformation', *Current Sociology*, 48 (4), 2000, pp. 1–13.

Institute of Public Policy Research (IPPR), 'Social Mobility: Special Issue', *New Economy*, 10, 2003.

Institute of Public Policy Research (IPPR), *The Family Report 2003: Choosing Happiness* (London, IPPR, 2004).

S. Irwin, 'The Changing Shape of Values, Care and Commitment', paper presented to ESPAnet Annual Conference – Changing European Societies: the Role of Social Policy, Copenhagen, 2003.

A. James and A. Prout, eds, *Constructing and Reconstructing Childhood: Contemporary Issues in the Sociological Study of Childhood* (London, Falmer, 1997).

L. Jamieson, *Intimacy: Personal Relationships in a Modern Age* (Cambridge, Polity Press, 1998).

A.M. Jensen and L. McKee, eds, *Children and the Changing Family: Between Transformation and Negotiation*, The Future of Childhood Series (London, Routledge/Falmer, 2003).

Joint Committee on Human Rights, *The Government's Response to the Committee's Tenth Report of Session 2002–2003 on the UN Convention on the Rights of the Child: Eighteenth Report of Session 2002–2003*, House of Lords Paper 187, House of Commons Paper 1279 (London, HMSO, 2003).

J.B. Kelly, 'Changing Perspectives on Children's Adjustment Following Divorce: A View from the United States', *Childhood*, 10 (2), 2003, pp. 237–54.

E.F. Kittay, 'A Feminist Public Ethic of Care Meets the New Communitarian Family Policy', *Ethics*, 111, 2001, pp. 523–47.

W. Langford, C. Lewis, Y. Solomon and J. Warin, *Family Understandings: Closeness, Authority and Independence in Families with Teenagers* (London, Family Policy Studies Centre in association with the Joseph Rowntree Foundation, 2001).

I. Levin, 'Living Apart Together: A New Family Form', *Current Sociology*, 52 (2), 2004, pp. 223–40.

J. Lewis, 'The Decline of the Male Breadwinner: Implications for Work and Care', *Social Politics*, 8 (2), 2001a, pp. 152–69.

J. Lewis, *The End of Marriage? Individualism and Intimate Relationships* (Cheltenham, Edward Elgar, 2001b).

R. Lister, 'Investing in the Citizen-Workers of the Future: Transformations in Citizenship and the State under New Labour', *Social Policy and Administration*, 37 (5), 2003, pp. 427–43.

W. Macpherson, *The Stephen Lawrence Inquiry*, Cm 4262-I (London, HMSO, 1999).

R. Mahon, 'Childcare: Towards What Kind of Social Europe?', *Social Politics*, 9 (3), 2002, pp. 343–79.

A. Marsh and J. Perry, *Family Change 1999–2001*, Research Report No. 180 (London, HMSO, 2003).

G. Martin and V. Kats, 'Families and Work in Transition in 12 Countries 1980–2001', *Monthly Labor Review Online*, September 2003, www.bls.gov/opub/mlr/2003/09/contents.htm

J. Mason, 'The Transnational Kinship Study: A Focus on Burial', CAVA Initial Findings Paper 2 (Leeds, CAVA, 2003), www.leeds.ac.uk/cava/papers/papers

J. Mason, 'Personal Narratives, Relational Selves: Residential Histories in the Living and Telling', *Sociological Review*, forthcoming, 2004.

S. McKay, *Working Families' Tax Credit in 2001*, Department of Work and Pensions Research Report No. 181 (Leeds, Department of Work and Pensions, 2003).

T. Modood, S. Beishon and S. Virdee, *Changing Ethnic Identities* (London, Policy Studies Institute, 1994).

D. Morgan, *Family Connections: An Introduction to Family Studies* (Cambridge, Cambridge University Press, 1996).

P. Morgan, *Farewell to the Family? Public Policy and Family Breakdown in Britain and the USA* (London, Institute for Economic Affairs Health and Welfare Unit, 1995).

P. Morgan, *Marriage Lite: The Rise of Cohabitation and its Consequences* (London, Institute for the Study of Civil Society, 2000).

J. Morris, *Pride Against Prejudice: A Personal Politics of Disability* (London, Women's Press, 1991).

J. Morris, *The Right Support: Report of the Taskforce on Supporting Disabled Adults in their Parenting Role* (York, York Publishing Services in association with the Joseph Rowntree Foundation, 2003).

P. Moss and P. Petrie, *From Children's Services to Children's Spaces: Public Policy, Children and Childhood* (London, Falmer, 2002).

J. Muncie, 'Institutionalized Intolerance: Youth Justice and the 1998 Crime and Disorder Act', *Critical Social Policy*, 19 (2), 1999, pp. 147–75.

C. Murray, *The Emerging British Underclass* (London, The Institute of Economic Affairs Health and Welfare Unit, 1990).

P.M. Nardi and B. Schneider, *Social Perspectives in Lesbian and Gay Studies: A Reader* (London, Routledge, 1998).

B. Neale, *Citizenship for Children: Strategies for Development* (York, Joseph Rowntree Foundation, 2003).

B. Neale, J. Flowerdew and C. Smart, 'Drifting Towards Shared Residence?', *Family Law*, 33, 2003, pp. 904–8.

B. Neale and C. Smart, 'Agents or Dependents? Struggling to Listen to Children in Family Law and Family Research', Working Paper 3 (University of Leeds, Centre for Research on the Family, Kinship and Childhood, 1998).

B. Neale and C. Smart, *Good to Talk? Conversations with Children about Divorce* (London, Young Voice, 2001).

B. Neale and C. Smart, 'Hard Choices? Re-Partnering after Divorce', *Sociology*, forthcoming, 2004.

B. Neale, A. Wade and C. Smart, '"I just get on with it": Children's Experiences of Family Life following Parental Separation or Divorce", Working Paper 1 (University of Leeds, Centre for Research on the Family, Kinship and Childhood, 1998).

M. O'Brien and I. Shemilt, *Working Fathers: Earning and Caring* (Manchester, Equal Opportunities Commission, 2003).

Office of National Statistics, *Social Trends 31* (London, HMSO 2001a).

Office of National Statistics, *Time Use Survey UK 2000* (London, HMSO, 2001b).

Office of National Statistics, *Social Trends 32* (London, HMSO 2002).

Office of National Statistics, *Census 2001: National Report for England and Wales* (London, HMSO, 2003a).

Office of National Statistics, *New Earnings Survey 2003* (London, HMSO, 2003b).

Office of National Statistics, *Social Trends 33* (London, HMSO 2003c).

Office of National Statistics, *Focus on Ethnicity* (London, HMSO, 2004a).

Office of National Statistics, *Labour Force Survey 2003* (London, HMSO, 2004b).

Office of National Statistics, *Living in Britain: Results from the General Household Survey 2002* (London, HMSO, 2004c).

Office of National Statistics, *Marriage, Divorce and Adoptions Statistics FM2 Series* (London, HMSO, 2004d).

Office of National Statistics, *Social Trends 34* (London, HMSO 2004e).

M. Oliver and C. Barnes, *Disabled People and Social Policy* (London, Longman, 1998).

R. Olsen and H. Clarke, *Parenting and Disability* (Bristol, Policy Press, 2003).

R. O'Neill, *Does Marriage Matter?* (London, Civitas, 2003).

Organisation for Economic Co-operation and Development (OECD), *Society at a Glance: OECD Social Indicators 2002 Edition* (Paris, OECD, 2003).

R. Pahl, *On Friendship* (Cambridge, Polity Press, 2000).

R. Pahl and L. Spencer, 'Personal Communities: Not Simply Families of "Fate" or "Choice"', *Current Sociology*, 52 (2), 2004, pp.199–221.

G. Palmer, J. North, J. Carr and P. Kenway, *Monitoring Poverty and Social Exclusion* (York, Joseph Rowntree Foundation, 2003).

A. Park, J. Curtice, K. Thomson, L. Jarvis and C. Bromley, eds, *British Social Attitudes: The 20th*

Report (London, Sage in association with the National Centre for Social Research, 2003).

T. Parsons, 'The Normal American Family', in B. Adams and T. Wierath, eds, *Readings on the Sociology of the Family* (Chicago, Markham, 1971).

A. Phillips, 'Why a Child is not a House', *The Guardian*, 17 October 2003.

K. Plummer, *Telling Sexual Stories: Power, Change and Social Worlds* (London, Routledge, 1995).

K. Quarmby, 'The Politics of Childcare', *Prospect*, 92, November 2003, pp. 50–5.

T. Reynolds, 'Analysing the Black Family', in A. Carling, S. Duncan and R. Edwards, eds, *Analysing Families: Morality and Rationality in Policy and Practice* (London, Routledge, 2002).

J. Ribbens-McCarthy and R. Edwards, 'The Individual in Public and Private: The Significance of Mothers and Children', in A. Carling, S. Duncan and R. Edwards, eds, *Analysing Families: Morality and Rationality in Policy and Practice* (London, Routledge, 2002).

J. Ribbens-McCarthy, R. Edwards and V. Gillies, *Making Families: Moral Tales of Parenting and Step-Parenting* (Durham, Sociology Press, 2003).

L. Richards and L. Ince, *Overcoming the Obstacles for Looked After Children: Quality Services for Black and Ethnic Minority Families and their Families* (London, The Family Rights Group, 2000).

L. Richards and R. Tapsfield, *Funding Families and Friends Care: The Way Forward* (London, The Family Rights Group, 2003).

S. Roseneil, 'Queer Frameworks and Queer Tendencies: Towards an Understanding of Postmodern Transformations of Sexuality', *Sociological Research Online*, 5 (3), 2000a.

S. Roseneil, 'Why we should Care about Friends', CAVA Workshop Paper (Leeds, CAVA, 2000b), www.leeds.ac.uk/cava/papers/workshoppapers.htm

S. Roseneil, 'We'd rather be with Friends', *New Statesman*, 15 December 2003.

S. Roseneil and S. Budgeon, 'Beyond the Conventional Family: Intimacy, Care and Community in the 21st Century', *Current Sociology*, 52 (2), 2004, pp. 135–59.

S. Roseneil and F. Williams, 'New Public Values of Parenting and Partnering: Voluntary Organisations and Welfare in New Labour's Britain', *Social Politics*, 11 (2), 2004, in press.

R. Sennett, *The Corrosion of Character: The Personal Consequences of Work in the New Capitalism* (New York/ London, WW Norton, 1999).

S. Sevenhuijsen, *Citizenship and the Ethic of Care: Feminist Considerations on Justice, Morality and Politics* (London, Routledge, 1998).

S. Sevenhuijsen, 'Caring in the Third Way', Working Paper 12 (University of Leeds, Centre for Research on the Family, Kinship and Childhood, 1999).

C. Shaw and J. Haskey, 'New Estimates and Projections of the Population Cohabiting in England and Wales', *Population Trends*, 95, 1999, pp. 8–19.

E.B. Silva and C. Smart, eds, *The New Family: The New Practices and Politics of Family Life* (London, Sage, 1999).

C. Smart, 'Divorce in England 1950–2000: A Moral Tale?', Working Paper Series 20 (University of Leeds, Centre for Research on the Family, Kinship and Childhood, 2000).

C. Smart, 'From Children's Shoes to Children's Voices', plenary given at the 25th Anniversary Conference of the Family Court of Australia, 2001.

C. Smart, 'Changing Landscapes of Family Life: Parents, Children and Divorce', paper presented at the National Council for One Parent Families Annual Conference 2003, London, November, 2003a.

C. Smart, 'Editor's Introduction: New Perspectives on Childhood and Divorce', *Childhood: Special Issue*, 10 (2), 2003b, pp. 123–254.

C. Smart, 'Landscapes of Family Life: Commitment and Ambivalence', public lecture presented at the University of Helsinki, Finland, 2003c.

C. Smart, 'Textures of Family Life: Further Thoughts on Change and Commitments', unpublished paper, 2004a.

C. Smart, 'Towards an Understanding of Family Change: Gender Conflict and Children's Citizenship', *Australian Journal of Family Law*, forthcoming, 2004b.

C. Smart, ed., 'New Perspectives on Childhood and Divorce', *Childhood: Special Issue*, 10 (2), 2003.

C. Smart and V. May, 'Residence and Contact Disputes in Court', *Family Law*, 34, 2004, pp. 36–42.

C. Smart and B. Neale, 'Experiments with Parenthood?', *Sociology*, 31 (2), 1997, pp. 201–29.

C. Smart and B. Neale, *Family Fragments?* (Cambridge, Polity Press, 1999).

C. Smart, B. Neale and A. Wade, 'Divorce and Changing Family Practices', Working Paper Series 11 (University of Leeds, Centre for Research on the Family, Kinship and Childhood, 1999).

C. Smart, B. Neale and A. Wade, *The Changing Experience of Childhood: Families and Divorce* (Cambridge, Polity Press, 2001).

C. Smart and R. Shipman, 'Visions in Monochrome: Some Problems of Theorising Contemporary Relationships', unpublished paper, 2004.

Social Security Advisory Committee, *Sixteenth Report: April 2002–July 2003* (London, HMSO, 2003).

J. Stacey, *In the Name of the Family: Rethinking Family Values in the Postmodern Age* (Boston, Beacon Press, 1996).

Strategy Unit, *Strategic Audit: Discussion Document* (London, Strategy Unit, 2003).

N. Tadmoor, *Family and Friends in the Eighteenth Century* (Cambridge, Cambridge University Press, 2001).

R. Thompson and J. Holland, 'Young People, Social Change and the Negotiation of Moral Authority', *Children and Society*, 16 (2), 2002, pp. 103–15.

J.C. Tronto, *Moral Boundaries: A Political Argument for an Ethic of Care* (New York, Routledge, 1993).

P. Toynbee, *Hard Work: Life in Low-Pay Britain* (London, Bloomsbury Publishing, 2003).

Trades Union Congress (TUC), *Childcare Review: TUC Response to HM Treasury 2004 Spending Review* (London, TUC/Daycare Trust, 2003).

C. Ungerson, 'Commodified Care Work in European Labour Markets', *European Societies*, 5 (4), 2003, pp. 377–96.

UK Coalition Against Poverty, *Listen Hear: The Right to be Heard. The Report of the Commission on Poverty, Participation and Power* (Bristol, Policy Press, 2000).

S. Vegeris and J. Perry, *Families and Children 2001: Living Standards*, Department of Work and Pensions Research Report No. 190 (Leeds, Department of Work and Pensions, 2003).

A. Wade and C. Smart, 'As Fair as it can be? Childhood after Divorce', in A. Jensen and L. McKee, eds, *Children and the Changing Family* (London, Routledge/Falmer, 2003).

J.S. Wallerstein and J.B. Kelly, *Surviving the Breakup: How Children and Parents Cope with Divorce* (London, Grant McIntyre, 1980).

J. Warin, Y. Solomon, C. Lewis and W. Langford, *Fathers, Work and Family Life* (York, Family Policy

Studies Centre in association with the Joseph Rowntree Foundation, 1999).

J. Weeks, B. Heaphy and C. Donovan, *Same Sex Intimacies: Families of Choice and Other Life Experiments* (London, Routledge, 2001).

K. Weston, *Families We Choose: Lesbians, Gay Men and Kinship* (New York, Columbia University Press, 1991).

C. Williams and J. Windebank, 'Helping People to Help Themselves: Policy Lessons from a Study of Deprived Urban Neighbours in Southampton', *Journal of Social Policy*, 29 (3), 2000, pp. 355–74.

F. Williams, *Social Policy: A Critical Introduction – Issues of 'Race', Gender and Class* (Cambridge, Polity Press, 1989).

F. Williams, 'Good-Enough Principles for Welfare', *Journal of Social Policy*, 28 (4), 1999, pp. 667–87.

F. Williams, 'In and Beyond New Labour: Towards An Ethic of Care', *Critical Social Policy*, 21 (4), 2001, pp. 467–93.

F. Williams, 'The Politics of Parenting and Partnering in Local Support Groups: Mobilisation, Care and Support', CAVA Initial Findings Paper 6 (Leeds, CAVA, 2003), www.leeds.ac.uk/cava/papers/papers

F. Williams, 'The Politics of Parenting and Partnering in Local Support Groups: Mobilisation, Care and Support', *Social Policy and Society*, forthcoming, 2004a.

F. Williams, 'Trends in Women's Employment, Domestic Service, and Female Migration: Changing and Competing Patterns of Solidarity', in T. Knijn and A. Komter, eds, *Solidarity Between the Sexes and Generations: Transformations in Europe* (Cheltenham, Edward Elgar, 2004b).

F. Williams, 'What Matters is who Works: Commentary on the Green Paper *Every Child Matters*', *Critical Social Policy*, 24 (3), 2004c, pp. 406–27.

F. Williams, J. Popay and A. Oakley, eds, *Welfare Research: A Critical Review* (London, UCL Press, 1999).

P. Willmott and M. Young, *The Symmetrical Family: A Study of Work and Leisure in the London Region* (London, Routledge and Kegan Paul, 1973).

J.Q. Wilson, *The Marriage Problem* (New York, HarperCollins, 2003).

Women and Equality Unit, *Responses to Civil Partnership: A Framework for the Legal Recognition of Same-Sex Couples* (London, Department of Trade and Industry, 2003).

S. Yeandle, 'Supporting Employed Carers: New Jobs, New Services?', paper presented at ESRC Seminar Series, The Interface Between Public Policy and Gender Equality, Sheffield Hallam University, 1999.

M. Young and P. Willmott, *Family and Kinship in East London* (London, Routledge and Kegan Paul, 1957).

Appendix 1   Policy landmarks for families and personal relationships: 1965–2003

Policies and Legislation	Key Effects
1965, 1968 and 1976 Race Relations Acts	The 1965 and 68 Acts outlawed direct discrimination in public places and services. Incitement to racial hatred was made a criminal offence. The 1976 Act extended the scope to indirect discrimination and placed a duty on local authorities to eliminate racism.
1967 Abortion Act	Gave women access to free and safe abortion within the NHS, conditional on particular grounds and the agreement of two doctors (excluding Northern Ireland).
1967 Sexual Offences Act	Decriminalised homosexuality between consenting adult males.
1969 Divorce Reform Act	Made no-fault divorce possible on the grounds of 'irretrievable breakdown' of the marital relationship and established the option of a two-year separation (or five-year non-consensual separation) while supporting traditional marital roles and responsibilities.
1971 and 1988 Immigration Acts	Restricted right of abode to 'patriality' – having a parent or grandparent born in the UK. The 1988 Act abolished the right of Commonwealth citizens to be joined by a spouse.
1974 Finer Report	Established the role of government in tackling poverty in lone parent households. Led to changes in the tax and benefit system in recognition of material disadvantage in these families.
1974 Equal Pay Act	Established the legal definition and procedures for equal pay for men and women doing the same or equivalent jobs in the same firm.
1984 Matrimonial and Family Proceedings Act	Enabled consensual divorce after one year and favoured 'clean break'.
1987 Family Law Reform Act	Abolished the status of illegitimacy; children born outside and inside of marriage were given equal rights (e.g. to maintenance, contact and inheritance). Unmarried fathers given the right to apply for parental responsibility.
1988 Local Government Act	Section 28 outlawed the promotion of homosexuality in any state-maintained school.
1989 Children Act	Established the child's best interests as paramount, and children as primarily their parents' responsibility – which cannot be voluntarily surrendered to the state. Following divorce parents are obliged to maintain their financial and care duties in the best interests of the child.
1989 United Nations Convention on the Rights of the Child	Contains 54 articles concerned with children's civil, economic, social and cultural rights. Established the right not to be discriminated against as the primary principle of this legislation as well as the protection of children's welfare and best interests.
1990 NHS and Community Care Act	Community and family care to be preferred over institutional care. Local authorities to be responsible for assessment and community care provision, and establishing a market of services supplied by voluntary, statutory and private providers.
1991 Child Support Act	Parents have primary responsibility to provide for their children. All absent parents to pay maintenance for their non-resident children as well as providing for second families. Child Support Agency established.

1995 Disability Discrimination Act	Established rights for disabled people not to be discriminated against in employment, or in the provision of services or premises.
1996 Family Law Act	Encouraged couples to take 'all practicable steps' to save a marriage before divorce (i.e. to undertake marriage guidance), but established that divorce should beof minimal distress and cost to all parties and children. Parents are obliged to maintain responsibilities and relationships to enhance their children's well-being. Increased protection against violence and abuse.
1997 Part-Time Work Directive	Part-time workers to receive no less favourable treatment than full-time workers in terms of training, pay, holidays, public holidays, access to pensions, sick pay and maternal or parental leave.
1998 Working Time Directive	European Directive stipulating a maximum working week of 48 hours and that workers had a right to three weeks' paid annual leave, rising to four weeks in November 1999.
1998 Social Security Act	Abolished the one parent premium in child benefit for lone parent families.
1998 New Ambitions for Our Country – A New Contract for Welfare Green Paper	Set out the new welfare contract which established paid work as the best route out of poverty. A programme of New Deals (for young unemployed, lone parents, older people, disabled people, people over 50) to be rolled out that offered incentives for those unemployed for over six months to take up paid work and training. The New Deal for Young People included compulsion to take up paid work or training or face benefit reductions.
1998 Supporting Families Consultation Document	Families to be supported in their diversity although marriage endorsed as the most stable family form for children. Set out parents' primary responsibility to children and the government's role in supporting marriage, employment and educational opportunities, and in extending family support services within health and welfare services.
1998–9 Sure Start Programme	Sure Start pre-school initiatives were rolled out targeting children under four at most risk from deprivation and poor schooling and including support for parents. The National Family and Parenting Institute set up to support all families and to carry out research into and promote best practice in supporting families within services. Parentline set up to offer support to all families.
1998 Human Rights Act	Set out a framework of human rights to protection, participation and provision.
1998 National Childcare Strategy; 1999 National Strategy for Carers	A framework for increasing childcare and early education places for three- and four-year-olds, initially in areas of deprivation and then for all children. The Carers' Strategy established a framework of provision for carers of older adults.
1999 Employment Relations and 2001 Employment Acts	Established a framework of maximum hours and extensions to maternity/paternity/adoption leave.
1999 Immigration and Asylum Act	Withdrew rights of asylum seekers to social security benefits and work permits.
1999 and 2001 Tax Credit Acts	Established a framework of tax credit for low-income earners with children administered through the Inland Revenue. Also available for childcare. Later extended to other low-earning adults.
2000 Carers and Disabled Children's Act	Local Authorities to assess the needs of and support carers.
2001 Race Relations Amendment Act	All public institutions to monitor their policies and practices for racial discrimination and to promote racial equality.
2003 Inter-Departmental Review of Childcare Strategy	Established the Ministry for Families, Young People and Children.
Proposals over 2003	*Every Child Matters* – a framework for reorganising child protection; universal services of family support. Consultation on Civil Partnerships – set out proposals for same-sex partnerships to be granted legal rights akin to marriage. Payments to informal carers for childcare – childcare tax credit payments to be granted to informal carers who are not family members. Section 28 repealed.

Appendix 2   Methodology of the CAVA research programme

The focus of the five-year CAVA research programme (1999–2004) was to examine – using in-depth qualitative research interviews – changes in parenting and partnering, and to consider the implications of these for future social policies. Research findings from six of the empirical projects in the programme are presented in Chapters 3 and 4. These are:

1. **Mothers, care and employment project:** how do partnered mothers with dependent children decide about taking up paid employment, about dividing labour with partners and about choosing childcare?
2. **Families after divorce project:** what happens to kin relationships after divorce?
3. **Transnational kinship project:** how are care commitments carried out when family members live in different countries or continents?
4. **Friendship and non-conventional partnership project:** how do people who live without a co-resident partner provide and receive care?
5. **Collective voices on care, diversity and family life project:** what 'claims' are being made by local and national groups and organisations about care, family lives and personal relationships?
6. **Values, care and commitments amongst parents of primary school children:** a survey in seven schools.

The first four projects all focused on a significant aspect of social change affecting family lives and personal relationships in Britain today – working mothers, divorce, migration and cultural diversity, and people living alone or without a co-resident partner. In-depth interviews (of approximately an hour to an hour and a half) were used with the aim of developing a nuanced and complex picture of the ways in which people cope with these changes and deal with the some of the dilemmas they create. In pursuing what it was that *mattered* to people in the situations in which they found themselves, we sought to develop a 'grounded and everyday' morality of family lives and personal relationships, and to add depth to the statistical picture of family change.

The samples for projects 1–4 and 6, and part of 5, were developed on the basis of a mapping exercise on the geography of family formations in the UK, conducted by Duncan and Smith.[1] This analysis used the 1991 British Census including the Sample of Anonymised Records, and the ONS Population and Vital Statistics. (This is discussed in Chapter 4 with reference to Duncan and Smith's follow-up analysis of the 2001 Census). Their analysis showed that it was possible to see that the variations in family formation which occur across the UK are also represented within Yorkshire and Lancashire. Second, it enabled us to draw our samples from different localities, not simply on the basis of conventional socio-economic variations but because they represented variations in family formations. Following this, six localities were chosen from which to draw our samples:

- **Craven:** a relatively well-off district council in the Yorkshire Dales centred around the commuting and retirement market towns of Skipton and Settle – strong representation of the 'traditional male breadwinner' family with high rates of births within marriage.
- **Barnsley:** a poor working-class town, hit by the collapse of coalmining which has also undermined the capacity for male breadwinning – traditional household divisions of labour, but also with high rates of births to cohabiting couples.
- **Burnley:** a poor working-class town hit by economic restructuring, but with an earlier history of female employment in the cotton industry – an 'adult worker' area with mothers more likely to be in full-time, paid employment, and also higher rates of births to cohabiting parents and of divorce, separation and lone parenthood.
- 'Transnational' **Bradford:** a working-class and ethnically diverse inner-city area, with higher than average proportions of residents who are international migrants, and who speak English as second language, together with second- and third-generation families of Eastern European and Pakistani origin – a high proportion of 'traditional' breadwinner families but, at the same time, with high rates of unconventional households.
- 'Alternative' **Leeds:** an inner-city zone polarised

between gentrifying areas of students and young professionals and ethnically diverse, working-class areas – high rates of alternative and unconventional households, side by side with high levels of traditional breadwinner families

• **Hebden Bridge:** in Calderdale District Council, a former mill town now gentrified by middle-class professionals and 'new age' residents – an adult worker area with high rates of births to cohabitants, and of gay and lesbian households.

Following ethnographic work, each project drew their sample, as appropriate to the subject matter, from these contrasting localities, along with class, gender, ethnic, cultural, sexual, household and other characteristics, where these were theoretically significant to their research questions. Overall, 396 individuals were interviewed as follows:

1. **Mothers, care and employment:** 40 interviews with working-class and middle-class white and African-Caribbean partnered mothers, 12 interviews with male partners and three focus groups in Barnsley, Burnley and Leeds. A further 60 parallel interviews distinguished by class, ethnicity and sexuality were available from Hebden Bridge and South London.

2. **Families after divorce:** 58 individuals representing 41 family clusters, including divorced parents and a member of kin group such as a grandparent, sibling or child, from Craven, Bradford and Leeds. Different faith/cultural backgrounds included Christian, Jewish, Muslim, Sikh and Hindu.

3. **Transnational kinship:** 69 individuals representing 17 family clusters with different generations within these clusters. Drawn from three 'migrant' communities: Pakistani in Bradford and Indian and Irish in Leeds. Interviews conducted in English and mother tongue.

4. **Friendship and non-conventional partnerships:** interviews with 53 individuals in Leeds, Barnsley and Hebden Bridge. Included gay and straight, living alone and sharing (with non-partners), white and African-Caribbean.

5. **Collective voices:** following a mapping exercise and pilot interviews, a sample of 23 national voluntary organisations and pressure groups and 14 trade unions was generated. A sample of 20 grass-roots self-help groups was similarly drawn from the localities. Semi-structured interviews were conducted with 62 key informants in the organisations.

6. **Values, care and commitments amongst parents of primary school children:** a survey of 102 parents in seven schools in contrasting school catchment areas within Leeds. Interviews conducted by HI Europe Research Consultancy.

The data from all but the last project were transcribed and entered into NVIVO (a qualitative analysis software package) and then coded and analysed. Interviews for the first four projects and the last were anonymised. 'Collective voices' interviewees were sent their transcripts with the option of signalling anything which they would not want to be publicly attributed to them.